OPPORTUNITIES

in

Building Construction Careers

OPPORTUNITIES

in

Building
Construction
Careers

REVISED EDITION

MICHAEL SUMICHRAST AND DAVID DAVITAIA

New York   Chicago   San Francisco   Lisbon   London   Madrid   Mexico City
Milan   New Delhi   San Juan   Seoul   Singapore   Sydney   Toronto

Library of Congress Cataloging-in-Publication Data

Sumichrast, Michael.
    Opportunities in building construction careers / by Michael Sumichrast. — Rev. ed.
      p.   cm.
    ISBN 0-07-148205-9 (alk. paper)
    1. Building trades—Vocational guidance—United States.   2. Construction
industry—Vocational guidance—United States.   I. Title.   II. Title: Opportunities in
building construction careers.

HD9715.U52S77   2007
690.023—dc22   2007010422

1 2 3 4 5 6 7 8 9 10 11 12 13 14 15 16 17 18 19   DOC/DOC   0 9 8 7

ISBN 978-0-07-148205-9
MHID   0-07-148205-9

Interior design by Rattray Design

McGraw-Hill books are available at special quantity discounts to use as premiums and
sales promotions, or for use in corporate training programs. For more information, please
write to the Director of Special Sales, Professional Publishing, McGraw-Hill, Two Penn
Plaza, New York, NY 10121-2298. Or contact your local bookstore.

This book is printed on acid-free paper.

CONTENTS

8. Issues and Trends

Safety. Women in construction. Systems-built
housing. Green building. A final word.

Preface

THE BUILDING TRADE is a great opportunity to establish a career and earn a living. I know; I started with a trade. I was a poor student and failed an entry exam for high school. My father used to say, "You will never amount to anything. All you do is play soccer and chase girls. I'm sending you to learn a trade."

And so he did. I worked three years in a metal-repair shop in a factory that employed three thousand people. We worked seven days a week from 6:00 A.M. to 2:00 P.M. On Sunday we got a break, working from 5:00 A.M. to 1:00 P.M. Five days a week we were required to attend school for two hours. I became proficient in machine mechanics. What a difference it made in my life! Any time I needed a job—in Europe, Australia, or the United States—I made good money by using my trade.

Even during the Eisenhower recession I found work. It didn't pay much: $1.00 per hour. But I had a job!

Eventually I attended high school and college, but I had to leave my country Czechoslovakia when the Communists took over in

1948. I enrolled in evening classes at Ohio State University while I worked as a construction superintendent building houses. It was difficult, but I earned my master's degree in business administration.

I continued to build houses until another recession shut down the housing industry. By that time I had already built about three thousand homes as a construction superintendent. My trade helped me to find a temporary job.

My advice to you is to earn your high school diploma. I know it can be hard, but nothing worth doing is easy. Then read this book. There are all kinds of possibilities open to you. Make up your mind to do it and stick to it.

Good luck!

1

CONSTRUCTION INDUSTRY

THE CONSTRUCTION INDUSTRY is vast indeed. Its 7.5 million workers account for about 19 percent of the nation's total employment and 9 percent of the total Gross National Product. It employs obvious workers such as carpenters, plumbers, and brick masons, as well as dozens of other trades workers that will be discussed in detail in later chapters.

For every dollar spent on direct construction, another two are spent on indirect expenditures. This "multiplier effect" means that for every construction project, additional funds are spent on a variety of items such as attorneys, financial services, government permit fees, real estate commissions, furniture, curtains, equipment, appliances, garden tools and plants, access roads, water and sewer extensions, and so on. These expenditures, combined with the actual construction costs, provide a welcome boost to the local economy.

In general, the construction industries in the United States and Canada are very similar. The major industry trends cross the border between the two countries, and there are few differences in wages as well.

A History of Progress

The construction industry in North America has made tremendous strides in the last fifty years. Evolutionary tools and mechanized earth-moving equipment have lifted it from pick-and-shovel primitiveness to a high degree of sophistication. Site development has become a science in itself, demanding the expertise of civil engineers as well as highly skilled operators using large and very expensive equipment. Maintenance of this equipment alone is an excellent, profitable, and rewarding trade or a profitable business on its own.

The cement industry has also contributed to this progress. We see proof of this every day in new superhighways, bridges, towering skyscrapers, and airway terminals. Speeding these developments has been the use of component parts. New factories use refinished walls, new offices use outside panels hoisted in place, new commercial or industrial buildings use inside curtain walls. Refinished applications are not limited to nonresidential use; much of the systems development is employed in residential construction, and this use will certainly increase in the future.

Today's buildings are very different from those constructed at the beginning of the twentieth century. Even a commercial or residential building erected only three or four decades ago is, in most cases, functionally obsolete by today's standards. Now there is more insulation, better drainage, and a greater variety of materials and equipment that did not exist a short time ago: garbage disposers, trash compactors, dishwashers, washers and dryers, air conditioners, humidifiers, air cleaners, and multiple garages.

Production engineering management of the construction process has become an integral part of this development. By use of processes such as the Critical Path Method—a technique that enables the user to think through a problem and create a logical, precise plan for its solution—yesterday's hit-and-miss planning and scheduling methods have been consigned to the junk heap.

Great improvements have been made in materials handling and packaging. For example, structural parts are stacked, wrapped, or taped in such a way that the parts flow readily into use from first to last. The entire package can be moved from truck to floor of the structure by machinery.

A whole sector of a structure is now mechanically handled and put in place on the site. Builders use forklift trucks, carryalls, bulldozers, tractors, graders, power shovels, backhoes, trenching wheels, and drilling and hole boring equipment. They also use electric saws, drills, staplers, routers, planers, nailing machines, electric power mixers, concrete and paint spray guns, small portable lifts, chain saws, and many other power tools to perform the many tasks involved in a construction project.

Organization

The industry is divided into different sectors, with various trades operating within each one. Home building, for instance, traditionally requires many carpenters, brick masons, plumbers, and electricians. Highway construction calls for a different composition of crews, as does the construction of high-rise office buildings.

The most recent data from the U.S. Bureau of Labor Statistics indicate that in 2004 there were a total of 818,000 establishments involved in construction. Of these, 247,000 were involved in the construction of buildings; 57,000 worked in heavy and civil engineering; and 514,000 were specialty trade contractors. Most of these establishments tend to be small, the majority employing fewer than five workers. About one out of nine workers are employed by small contractors.

These numbers indicate the prevalence of the subcontracting system, which allows for division of labor, diversification of responsibilities, use of credit, reduction in working capital that would otherwise be needed for direct employment of many people, and freedom from the need to purchase and store materials in one huge central depot. To reinforce this point, a survey by the National Association of Home Builders of its builder members reports that more than two-thirds use subcontractors in residential construction projects.

Ownership and Employment

Construction is one of the nation's largest industries, with 7.0 million wage and salary jobs and 1.9 million self-employed and unpaid family workers in 2004. Almost two out of three salaried jobs in construction were with specialty trade contractors, primarily plumbing, heating, and air-conditioning; electrical; and masonry contractors. Around one out of four jobs were with building contractors, mostly in residential and nonresidential construction. The rest were with heavy and civil engineering construction contractors.

Construction offers more opportunities than most other industries for individuals who want to own and run their own business.

The 1.9 million self-employed and unpaid family workers in 2004 performed work directly for property owners or acted as contractors on small jobs, such as additions, remodeling, and maintenance projects. The rate of self-employment varies greatly by individual occupation in the construction trades.

Statistics Canada reports that at the start of the millennium there were 218,746 construction companies, most of which were small- and medium-sized enterprises with fewer than five employees. Geographically, most of these firms were based in four provinces. Ontario had the largest number, with the Toronto area serving as the hub of construction activity in Canada, followed by Quebec, British Columbia, and Alberta. The largest numbers of these companies operated in the residential construction, electrical, plumbing and equipment installation, exterior finishing, and interior finishing sectors.

Construction: Private and Public

The construction industry functions in two sectors—private and public—each of which has its own subdivisions. The private sector is divided into residential, nonresidential, farm, public utilities, and other. The public sector comprises buildings (residential, industrial, educational, medical, and other public structures), highways, military facilities, conservation and development, and other public facilities.

Private Construction

Private construction totaled nearly $931 billion in 2006 and accounted for about 78 percent of total construction expenditures.

The largest single individual subcategory is the construction of residential buildings. Although the proportion of residential construction varies from year to year, it accounts for an average of 45 to 52 percent of the total U.S. private construction activity, and in July 2006 it reached 52.3 percent.

In residential construction, approximately 35 percent of the work was in new housing units; the majority involved additions and alterations to existing buildings. Expenditures for nonresidential buildings accounted for 25.3 percent of total construction activity. The commercial sector accounted for about half of all nonresidential private construction, followed by the industrial sector.

Residential construction is the largest single segment among the various types of construction activities. It includes construction of new single-family housing units, multiple units (apartments and condominiums), additions to existing buildings, alterations, and expenditures for so-called "nonhousekeeping" buildings, which include lodge associations or club building with bedrooms, rooming houses, dormitories, and fraternity houses.

Most residential construction is privately financed, with only about 2 or 3 percent directly financed by public funds. Nineteen percent of the new units built annually are insured or guaranteed by the Federal Housing Administration (FHA) or the Veterans Administration (VA). Funds for these FHA and VA units, however, come out of the private rather than public lending sector. From the end of World War II to 2006, more than 102.8 million housing units were built.

Public Construction

Public construction outlays were $269.1 billion in July 2006 and centered mainly in highway and street construction, sewer systems, and buildings for educational purposes. Expenditures for highways and streets account for about 7 percent of all construction, or about one-third of total public expenditures. Sewer systems registered a 1.5 percent share of the total, while educational building consumed another 3.7 percent. Residential building under the public sector is small, about 0.7 percent. Similarly, expenditures for industrial construction amount to about 0.7 percent. Conservation and development account for about 1 percent of the total expenditures.

Today's Houses

Today's houses are quite different from those built thirty to forty years ago. To begin with, they are substantially larger and contain more conveniences and more labor-saving devices. An average house built in 1980 was about 1,700 square feet. By 2000 the average square footage had increased to 2,265, and in 2006 it was 2,500. Very few two-bedroom units are built for sale today; the majority of new homes have at least three bedrooms and two or more bathrooms. Sale prices have more than doubled, but this is not necessarily because of inflation. Today's house has more in it, is much larger and better built, and rests on more expensive land.

Residential construction has gone through many evolutionary changes in the last seventy years. Many building materials are now precut or prefabricated, saving builders considerable time. There is a significant division of labor and, with it, increased responsibilities for each small operation. Today's builders are businesspeople rather than old-line construction bosses, who once came mostly from the ranks of a trade. And the new breed uses new techniques in managerial skills, planning, forecasting, scheduling, and control devised by the use of automatic processing equipment.

The changes in residential construction have affected more than the building of houses. Builders have become more involved in community development and marketing their projects. There is more sophistication in the approach to the consumer, more technique in advertising, promotion, and selling. There is greater emphasis on consumer satisfaction and anticipation of buyers' expectations. Builders in suburban areas are likely to construct subdivisions consisting of a number of individual houses; some include a few houses, while others number in the hundreds. In the exurbs, which are generally more rural and farther away from a city center, builders may plan a community that includes recreational facilities, schools, shopping, churches, and cultural centers.

Outlook for Residential Construction

People and places are the essential ingredients of a thriving, expanding construction industry. The housing needs of people are enormous today and will continue to be in the years ahead.

In the past forty years, the number of new households has increased on average 1.3 million in each decade. Although household growth is expected to slow slightly over the coming decade, the increase will create demand for residential construction in the United States, especially in the fastest-growing areas in the South and West. The demand for homes and rental apartments will be spurred by the rising numbers of immigrants, as well as the children of baby boomers. In addition, a desire for larger homes with more amenities will fuel demand for move-up homes, as well as the renovation and expansion of older homes. Townhouses and condominiums in conveniently located suburban and urban settings also are increasingly desired types of properties.

Canada's Construction Sector Council projects a cooling trend in the overall industry, led by a small decline in residential construction. The residential sector is expected to begin recovery in 2008 and should experience growth of 2.3 percent in 2009.

New housing construction, of course, triggers construction activity of all sorts—schools, highways, commercial establishments, retail stores, shopping centers, gas stations, small and large grocery stores. As our producing capacity of consumer goods is enlarged, we will need new factories, dams, canals, water transportation, and gas and electric lines to support residential construction.

Housing is the single most important item in the national economy. Although the real estate downturn that began in 2006 will have an impact, the fact remains that people continue to need housing. The industry might see fewer teardowns and construction of very large homes, but smaller, more affordable units will continue to be built. In addition, more emphasis will be placed on rebuilding and rehabilitating existing residences. This rebuilding is the thrust of current government policies, and the existing inventory is quite large compared to new production. Much wealth is accumulated in these units, and expenditures for their upkeep and improvement are already approaching expenditures for new residential construction. As a matter of fact, during a housing crisis the renovation of existing housing usually soars upward while new housing declines.

Nonresidential Construction

More than $559 million was spent on nonresidential buildings in 2006. Of this, $80.7 million was spent on commercial buildings, and $125.8 million on health care and educational buildings. About $75 million was spent on highway and street construction.

Health-related facilities constituted a large percentage of nonresidential construction, as hospitals expanded and established satellite facilities. In addition, technological advances have led to the construction of more diagnostic laboratories and research facilities than ever before.

The construction of educational buildings continues to gain strength, particularly in suburban areas. As more people move to suburbs and exurbs, school systems are rapidly adding new buildings and approving major renovations of existing structures.

Outlook for Nonresidential Construction

We have considered the changes in the size of houses over the last fifty years. As basic shelter requirements changed, so have those for nonresidential construction. For example, neighborhood shopping centers now require up to ten acres and regional shopping centers up to one hundred acres, compared with only about one-third of this space forty years ago.

Overall, nonresidential construction is expected to grow faster over the next decade than residential construction. Replacement of many industrial plants has been delayed for years, and a large number of structures will have to be replaced or remodeled. Many of these are now being located on larger areas of land outside of cities. Instead of the bleak, depressing monolithic structures built forty-five years ago, today they are usually one- and two-story buildings in pleasantly landscaped surroundings.

Construction of nursing homes and other residential homes for the elderly, as well as all types of health-care facilities, will be necessary to meet the need for more medical treatment facilities, especially by the growing elderly population. Construction of schools will continue to be needed, especially in the South and West, as this is where the population is growing the fastest. In other areas, however, replacing and renovating older schools will create more jobs. New and renovated educational facilities have also changed drastically. More space now is provided not only for classrooms but for parking, dormitories, and sports and recreation facilities as well. And with the increasing use of distinctive architectural designs and vivid colors, today's schools look much less institutional than do those that were built in the past.

Employment in heavy and civil engineering construction is projected to increase due to growth in new highway, bridge, and street construction, as well as in maintenance and repairs to prevent further deterioration of the nation's existing highways and bridges. America's mobile population has demanded construction of new airports around more cities and towns, yet air traffic becomes more congested and more and larger airports are necessary.

In Canada, the nonresidential construction industry experienced a boom year in 2006, recording record growth of 7.2 percent. However, this growth is expected to cool down progressively in the years ahead, with projections of 2.2 percent in 2008, 1.2 percent in 2009, and then a drop by 0.3 percent in 2010.

Within the nonresidential sector, the leading subsectors in 2007 will include engineering construction and industrial construction, following on the strong gains made by both these subsectors in 2006. Both commercial and institutional/government construction are expected to post gains in 2007, but not at the same rate as engineering and industrial.

Opportunities for Employment

Given the size of the construction industry and the variety of skills it encompasses, there are many opportunities for employment in this challenging field, and the overall outlook is excellent. For one thing, many employees are expected to retire in the next decade, and new, young workers will be needed to fill their positions.

Until only a relatively few years ago, the industry was tied to the seasons, generally local in nature, and subject to a high turnover in the workforce. But new technologies, both on-site and off-site, are beginning to remove the seasonal risks and the possibilities of unemployment during bad weather, thus creating more year-round employment.

Employment Outlook

The number of wage and salary jobs in the construction industry is expected to grow about 11 percent through the year 2014, compared with 14 percent that is projected for all industries combined. This increase depends primarily on the level of construction and remodeling activity, which is expected to increase over the coming decade.

Employment should grow fastest in specialty trades contracting, the largest segment of the industry. This will be the result of demand for subcontractors in building and heavy construction and for more workers needed to repair and remodel existing homes, which specialty trade contractors are more likely to perform. Home improvement and repair construction is expected to continue to grow faster than new home construction, and remodeling should be the fastest-growing sector of housing construction because of a growing stock of old residential and nonresidential buildings.

The number of job openings in construction may fluctuate from year to year, because new construction is usually cut back during periods when the economy is not expanding or interest rates are high. However, it is rare that all segments of the construction industry are down at the same time, allowing workers to switch from building houses to working on office building construction, depending on demand.

Employment growth will differ among the various occupations and trades. For example, employment of construction managers is expected to grow as a result of the increasing complexity of projects that need to be managed, including dealing with the proliferation of laws regulating building construction, worker safety, and environmental issues. Also, the opportunity for self-employment in this industry is leading a larger number of managers to open small construction businesses. An especially favorable job outlook is expected for those with a bachelor's degree in construction science with an emphasis on construction management, and for those with related work experience in construction management services firms.

Although employment in construction trades as a whole is expected to grow about as fast as the industry average, the rate of growth will vary by trade, depending on the demand for a trade at any given time.

After a number of years of significant employment growth, construction employment in Canada is expected to level off in 2007. After growth rates of 7.1 percent in 2005 and 2.7 percent in 2006, growth in the construction labor force will slow to 0.9 percent in 2007 and will rebound 1.4 percent in 2008. However, over the next ten years the industry will need to replace more than 150,000 retiring workers, or 19 percent of the current workforce, leading to many new job opportunities.

Union Membership

The North American construction industry in general is unionized, with the exception of the home building sector. While more than 75 percent of general construction workers are members of local affiliates of the seventeen AFL-CIO building trades unions, it is likely that fewer than half of the workers in the home building industry are covered under collective bargaining agreements.

For those who plan to work as union members, the preferred method for learning a trade and entering the industry is through apprenticeships. However, many do become skilled workers without formal training. In the apprenticeship method, national standards have been developed by the Bureau of Apprenticeship and Training in consultation with international unions. These programs are coordinated with local joint labor-management committees that also develop admission standards. Generally, such standards require that an applicant be between the ages of seventeen and twenty-five and have from nine to twelve years of education. More detailed information about apprenticeships is given in the following chapters. Vocational education courses also supply a good number to the pool of skilled workers in the construction industry.

Jobs for Young People

For many teenagers, having a job in the summer is as customary as cookouts and family vacations. More than half of those aged sixteen to nineteen were employed in July 2005, the month that marks the height of youth employment.

About 383,000 of these young people found work in construction. Although not all will pursue construction as a career, a summer job is an excellent way to learn a trade. Most teens start as laborers or helpers, with responsibilities that include moving materials, cleaning up the work site, and assisting experienced workers.

If there are construction projects under way in your area, inquire about possible temporary employment as a helper. Many young people find summer jobs through relatives who work in a trade, so don't be afraid to ask people you know in the field if they might be able to recommend you for a job.

2

Training and Education Programs

A VARIETY OF training and education options are available for those interested in a career in building construction. From college programs to apprenticeships offered by trade unions to alternative programs sponsored by national organizations, you can find a level of training that suits your needs and helps to prepare you for a career in this exciting field.

Apprenticeship Programs

Many workers enter the construction trades through apprenticeship programs. Administered by local employers, trade associations, and trade unions, these programs provide the most thorough training in their respective trades. They are designed to meet national standards that are established by the unions in conjunction with federal requirements.

Apprenticeships usually last between three and five years and consist of on-the-job training combined with 144 hours or more of related classroom instruction each year. A number of apprenticeship programs now use competency standards in place of time requirements, making it possible to complete a program in a shorter time.

To enroll in most apprenticeship programs, you must be at least seventeen or eighteen years old and in good physical condition. Some graduates of technical or vocational schools who go on to apprenticeship training progress at a somewhat faster pace, because they have already taken courses such as mathematics, mechanical drawing, and woodworking.

Trade unions are perhaps the best sources of information about apprenticeship programs. Bear in mind that for many unions, you must be sponsored or recommended for membership by a current member. If you know someone who is a member of the union you wish to join, it's a good idea to ask him or her about the possibility of becoming your sponsor and recommending you for entry into a training program. While working as an apprentice, you are a member of the union and are covered by its collective bargaining agreement. You must also abide by all union rules and regulations.

For a list of trade unions and contact information, please see Appendix B. Note that the unions listed serve members in both the United States and Canada. Links to provincial apprenticeship opportunities can be found at the website of the Canadian Home Builders Association, at www.chba.ca.

Sample Apprenticeship Program

As an example of an apprenticeship program, let's examine the requirements and elements of the program offered to apprentice carpenters.

Apprenticeship applicants must generally be at least seventeen years old and meet the requirements of the local union. For example, some union locals test an applicant's aptitude for carpentry; the length of the program, usually about three to four years, varies based on the apprentice's skill. Applicants must be physically able to perform the work of the trade and must meet any other qualifications set forth by the local.

Terms of Apprenticeship

As in most trades, an apprenticeship in carpentry is measured in hours and requires approximately eight thousand hours or four years, with eight six-month periods of reasonably continuous employment. Classroom attendance for at least 144 hours per year is mandatory. An applicant can receive credit for previous practical experience and may be granted advanced standing based on prior qualifications. An apprentice works the same number of regular hours as a journeyman but cannot work overtime if it interferes with class attendance. Once an apprentice has passed the journeyman examination, he or she is awarded a certificate issued by a registered agency. The primary components of a carpentry apprenticeship are as follows:

Layout	500 hours
Form building	1,200 hours
Rough framing	1,200 hours
Outside finishing	800 hours
Inside finishing	1,500 hours
Care and use of tools	500 hours
Welding	500 hours
Plastic and resilience	300 hours

Acoustics and resilience	1,000 hours
Miscellaneous	500 hours
Total	8,000 hours

In addition, apprentices study the ethics and history of the carpentry trade, tools and materials of the trade, and review and application of basic mathematics. They also study such related skills as elementary blueprint reading, foundations, roof framing, stair building and finishing, and cabinet making.

Vocational, Technical, and College Courses

More than fourteen hundred colleges, universities, trade schools, and vocational schools offer programs in construction throughout the United States. In Canada, more than sixty schools offer certificates, diplomas, and degrees in aspects of construction.

The many trade and vocational schools offer widely varying numbers of courses in the construction trades. At the high school level, shop courses in wood, metal, electric, and heating all provide a good foundation for progression to a commercial trade school and an eventual union apprenticeship.

Students can enter a trade school with a high school diploma or its equivalent. Many older students who have served in the military enter trade schools with experience in a trade such as carpentry, electrical work, or any of the other specialty trade areas.

Increasing numbers of colleges are offering bachelor's degrees in construction. These programs are generally aimed toward the student who intends to move up into construction management. Undergraduate students study construction materials and take courses in methods, structures, environmental systems, and construction management courses.

Students at the graduate level can pursue a master of science in building construction or master of science in construction management. Graduate programs vary to some degree in content, but in general they offer similar core programs with varying related elective courses, often depending on the strength of various related departments in the college or university.

To find a construction education program in the United States, visit www.uscollegesearch.org, where you can search for schools by location or degrees offered. To locate programs in Canada, visit www.schoolfinder.com. Both sites offer information about financial aid and career guidance.

Alternative Training Programs

In addition to the training opportunities mentioned above, there are a number of alternative programs offered by a variety of sources.

The Home Builders Institute

The Home Builders Institute (HBI) was established in 1983 as the workforce development branch of the National Association of Home Builders (NAHB). The creation of this nonprofit corporation was a result of the merger of NAHB's Manpower Development and Training Division, Education Department, and the Education Foundation.

The HBI is one of a long list of educational endeavors undertaken by NAHB. In the 1940s, the organization began offering seminars for members and introduced residential construction training in 1967 when it was awarded its first contracts with the federal government. In 1970 NAHB began Operation Transition, a training program for Vietnam veterans interested in pursuing careers in brick masonry. Four years later, HBI's partnership with the U.S. Department of Labor and its Job Corps program began, training young people in the trades at the Woodstock Job Corps Center in Maryland.

Estimates from the Department of Labor (DOL) suggest that by 2015 more than one million new jobs will be created to meet America's construction demands. In response, DOL gave HBI a grant through the President's High Growth Job Training Initiative to increase participation in trades training. The grant aims to recruit twenty-five hundred people into the residential construction industry by providing quality trades training and an associate's degree or equivalent in the applied sciences. Home builders associations in ten states are spearheading the program in partnership with local school boards, community colleges, and workforce development boards.

As the number of jobs in residential construction continues to grow, so, too, does the variety of jobs within the building industry. In January 2006, HBI launched a career recruitment and awareness campaign for the twenty-first century. The "Make It Happen" campaign uses posters, brochures, and multimedia to inform students, parents, and educators of the multitude of careers that are available in home building. Visit the Make It Happen website, www.build ingcareers.org, for information about the campaign and links to resources for education and careers in the building construction industry.

Trades Training for Youth and Adults

Pre-apprenticeship and apprenticeship training in residential construction are offered through HBI's training programs. These programs are public/private partnerships of national, state, and local agencies concerned about the nation's shortage of construction craft workers. Faced with the need for long-term career training solutions, these agencies have entered into a partnership with the home building industry through HBI.

HBI's training programs employ comprehensive curricula developed by members of the housing industry to combine academic instruction and hands-on training on actual construction projects. Participants also learn literacy and employability skills. Following are brief descriptions of current HBI training programs.

Project CRAFT (Community, Restitution, Apprenticeship-Focused Training)

This program uses a comprehensive educational approach to help troubled young people turn their lives around and gain sustainable employment in the building industry. Students spend an average of 840 hours in training over a six-month period, with 25 percent of the time in classroom-related instruction and 75 percent in a community service/work-based learning environment that combines classroom learning with work site experience. CRAFT students generally work toward a GED or high school diploma while completing HBI's Pre-Apprenticeship Certificate Training (PACT). Under the supervision of industry-experienced instructors, students learn residential construction skills while completing community service construction projects.

Project TRADE (Training, Restitution, Apprenticeship, Development, and Education)

Designed to train and place adult ex-offenders, the program operates in selected states by providing participants with the training to secure employment. Community service construction projects are the gateway for helping offenders to reintegrate into society.

HUD Youthbuild Partnership

The partnership of HBI and the U.S. Department of Housing and Urban Development's Youthbuild offers low-income youth access to industry-sponsored vocational training and the opportunity for a career in the home-building industry. Participants receive a combination of classroom academic instruction, job skills development, and on-site training in a construction trade. With support from HUD, they use their newly acquired skills to rehabilitate and build housing for low-income and homeless people in their communities.

Project HOPE (Home-Building Opportunities for Positive Employment)

The goal of this program is to offer trades training and job placement services to people with disabilities. HBI works with local home-building associations to merge the needs of vocational rehabilitation clients with the workforce needs of the housing industry.

Project CRAFT SKILLS (Community Reintegration Apprenticeship-Focused Training, Seniors Keeping Intensive Life Long Skills)

Established in collaboration with the National Council on Aging (NCOA), this program trains and places workers ages fifty-five and above in facilities maintenance.

Project HEART (Homeless Employment and Related Training)

The program aims to train and place homeless men and women in the residential construction industry.

Doors to Success

Funded by the U.S. Department of Labor's Office of Veterans Employment and Training Services, this program helps female veterans transition to new careers in housing.

Job Corps Program

Sponsored by the U.S. Department of Labor, Job Corps is the United States' oldest and largest residential education and job training program for at-risk youth. For the past forty years, the Home Builders Institute has partnered with Job Corps, training and placing more than two thousand young people annually in the residential construction industry.

HBI offers trades training programs at sixty-seven Job Corps campuses in forty states and the District of Columbia. Students study the following trades: brick masonry, carpentry, electrical wiring, facilities maintenance, landscaping, painting, and plumbing.

Job Corps graduates have a minimum of eight hundred hours of hands-on training in a real work environment, a driver's license, trade clothing and tools, and knowledge of the proper and safe use of hand and power tools. They are also prescreened prior to an initial employment interview.

HBI places Job Corps graduates in every state, and many students choose to relocate for available jobs. The program provides employers with a reliable source of skilled entry-level workers.

Employers can streamline their hiring process and decrease costs of on-the-job training, accidents, and absenteeism.

Available Training

Students receive training in eight construction trades with curricula that are regularly updated and industry-validated. In the course of their training, Job Corps students also complete construction projects for their community, which means HBI Job Corps students, before their first day on the job, have been on real work sites with real deadlines.

HBI Job Corps students learn the following skills:

- **Brick masonry.** Students learn how to professionally mix mortar; lay block and brick; build safe scaffolds; construct fireplaces, arches, and patios; lay out building lines; lay brick floors and stairs; and operate a diamond blade brick saw.
- **Carpentry.** Carpentry students learn to build walls and forms for concrete; lay roofs with plywood and shingles; build and set cabinets and counters; install doors, windows, and siding; install roof joists, rafters, and trusses; lay wood floors; and operate table saws, power drills, and nail guns.
- **Electrical wiring.** Students studying this trade learn how to cut, bend, and install conduit and wiring; hook up electrical appliances; install switches and lighting fixtures; wire door bells and alarms; and use circuit-testing equipment.
- **Facilities maintenance.** Skills learned in this trade include the ability to replace windows, doors, plumbing, and electrical fixtures; repair floor tile and carpet; maintain landscaped areas and all types

of floor, wall, and ceiling surfaces; frame and install drywall; and use and repair hand and power tools.

   • **Landscaping.** Landscaping students learn to grade and prepare soil for planting; identify, plant, transplant, prune, and care for trees, shrubs, and flowers; seed, edge, rake, and treat lawns; install retaining walls, fences, and bed borders; and safely operate equipment such as mowers, tractors, trimmers, and chain saws.

   • **Painting.** Students in the painting trade learn to prepare surfaces such as wood, drywall, plaster, and masonry; know the difference between water- and oil-based paints; work with airless and conventional spray systems; apply stains, finishes, and wall coverings; and sand and water-blast surfaces.

   • **Plumbing.** Students learn to cut and install pipes and fittings; install fixtures such as sinks, dishwashers, and disposals; repair and test water lines; install water heaters; work with adhesives and hand tools such as saws and plumbing wrenches; and operate power tools such as pipe threaders and solder torches.

Who Are Job Corps Students?

Job Corps students are motivated learners and workers who voluntarily enroll in the program. To be eligible, a young person must be:

   • Between sixteen and twenty-four years old
   • Economically disadvantaged
   • Not on probation or parole
   • Free of serious medical or behavioral problems
   • Willing to sign a commitment to be free of violence and drugs

- Motivated and capable to succeed in Job Corps
- A high-school dropout or a person in need of education and training to obtain and hold meaningful employment
- A U.S. citizen or lawfully admitted alien

Young people enroll in Job Corps because they want to work, and they agree to abide by the program's rules to reach their goal of self-sufficiency. For more information on enrolling in the home building trades in Job Corps, select the "Training Opportunities" link at www.hbi.org.

Continuing Education Programs

The Home Builders Institute and the National Association of Home Builders offer a number of continuing education options for construction professionals.

HBI offers two continuing educational opportunities for those who wish to advance in the industry of building construction.

Residential Construction Superintendent

The residential construction superintendent (RCS) designation is geared toward field superintendents, administrative personnel, trade foremen, builders, and anyone elsewishing to excel in this position. Eight courses cover issues and subjects identified by National Association of Home Builder members as being critical to a field supervisory job. The curriculum covers the following core competencies:

- **General project management.** Managing production operations through the planning, action, and review (PAR) method as well as understanding estimates. This course is designed to provide an overview of the many different facets of being a superintendent.

• **Planning and scheduling.** Methods of improving planning and scheduling skills to increase profits, effectiveness, and on-time deliveries. The course covers five fundamental scheduling methods necessary for the successful management of a project.

• **Budget management and cost control.** Impacting the profitability of the company. Learn the importance of the superintendent's role regarding profitability, as well as how to control the critical elements of job costs. The course also includes tips on identifying the costs to everyone when a job is not done right the first time.

• **Customer service and home owner relations.** Understanding the human and business needs of customers. Students learn how to meet and exceed expectations by avoiding the "seven deadly sins" of customer service, as well as how to effectively deal with difficult customers.

• **Safety and security.** Protecting the job site by learning the essential components of a safety program. The course examines the most common Occupational Safety and Health Administration (OSHA) citations and how to prepare for an OSHA inspection, and reviews a superintendent's responsibilities to adequately protect the job site.

• **Codes and quality control.** Learning to define quality by identifying five essential quality components that help to set performance expectations. This course outlines a superintendent's responsibilities regarding codes and provides tips on how to enforce code compliance on the job site.

• **Hiring, training, and supervision.** Examining the common mistakes made during the interview process and learning the necessary steps to ensure that each subcontractor and/or employee is the right fit for the company. In addition, tips and tools for setting and measuring performance expectations are explored.

• **Office and subcontractor relations.** Learning to spot promising characteristics in job site workers as well as how to recruit successful subcontractors for the job. This course also offers tips for creating a positive partnership with internal customers and provides a strategy for dealing with conflict.

Advanced Residential Construction Superintendent Designation

In response to demand from members, instructors, and students for additional training, HBI is currently developing a second and advanced track of RCS programming—the Advanced Residential Construction Superintendent (ARCS) designation.

Designed for professionals who have already received their RCS designation, ARCS covers more specific topics in the rapidly expanding world of residential construction supervision.

The ARCS series consists of three tracks of specialized courses. At the time of this writing, the following courses are available in each track:

Professional Growth Track

• **Blueprint for Effective Communication.** Participants will learn to identify the necessary components of the communication process, explore methods to minimize the barriers to effective communication, and practice ways to use their communication style to improve customer relationships.

• **Collaborating with Challenging Customers.** This course explores the motivation behind the challenging customer's behavior. It provides tools and techniques to effectively cope with this behavior and satisfy the customer's needs while retaining composure and professionalism. Participants will identify four of the most common challenging customers and develop a road map for productive customer service interactions.

Building Leaders Track

• **Managing Conflict on the Job Site.** This course is designed to develop, enhance, and maintain productive relationships on the job site between superintendents, trade contractors, and customers. Participants will explore the roots of potential conflict, define the stages, and identify methods to control escalation. The last section of the course focuses on identifying and practicing the "directing differences" technique of conflict resolution so participants can use these tools to prevent and/or manage conflict when it occurs.

• **Coaching and Creating Standards of Excellence.** The goal of this course is to develop and improve coaching skills so that leaders can motivate and provide support to achieve top performance. Participants will define coaching, explore the characteristics of great coaching, and utilize a three-step process to ensure effective coaching conversations.

Technical Proficiency Track

• **Quality Construction.** This course aims to improve quality construction in the homebuilding industry by identifying and developing best practices. It identifies the stakeholders of a construction project and the performance expectations that need to be set and measured for each group to ensure product quality. Participants will also learn technical tips and best practices to improve quality at each stage of a construction project.

• **Running a Successful Job: Job Site Best Practices.** This course identifies the components of a successful job so that superintendents can improve the home-building process and achieve product quality and on-time delivery. It lists the three essential skills of successful superintendents and outlines how to use them for effective project management. Participants discuss and review best job site practices so the job is done right the first time and learn how to effectively implement emergency procedures by utilizing a three-step process.

Since the ARCS designation is still in development, you should visit www.hbi.org for the most current course offerings.

NAHB offers several designations for construction professionals. Following are descriptions of the main programs and their requirements.

Certified Graduate Associate

This first step in professional designations is earned through classroom instruction taught by experienced builders and remodelers. It affirms your level of industry knowledge and your commitment to your professionalism in the building industry.

An applicant for the certified graduate associate (CGA) designation must meet the following course requirements:

Required Courses
• Business Management for Building Professionals
• Customer Service
• Sales and Marketing or Sales and Marketing for Remodelers

Electives (Three)

- Building Codes and Standards
- Building Technology: Structures and Exterior Finishes
- Building Technology: Systems and Interior Finishes
- Business Accounting and Job Cost
- Construction Contracts and Law
- Design/Build
- Energy Efficient Construction
- Estimating
- Finance Banking
- Green Building for Building Professionals
- Indoor Air Quality
- Insurance Reconstruction
- Land Development, Site Planning, and Zoning
- Negotiating Skills
- Off-Site Project Management
- On-Site Project Management
- Quality Construction
- Scheduling

A further requirement is the completion of twelve hours of continuing education every three years. At least six hours must come from a National Association of Home Builders University of Housing course.

Certified Graduate Builder

In order to apply for the Certified Graduate Builder (CGB) designation, a candidate must already have had at least two years of building industry experience by the time he or she has completed the program, and that individual must take the Builder Assessment Review (BAR), which determines what courses he or she must complete to earn the Certified Graduate Builder designation. Existing candidates who do not take the Builder Assessment Review must complete nine courses to obtain the designation. The results of the Builder Assessment Review will list the number of courses required (from no courses to two) from the key areas of the designation curriculum:

Building Technology
- Building Codes and Standards
- Building Technology: Structures and Exterior Finishes
- Building Technology: Systems and Interior Finishes
- Energy Efficient Construction
- Green Building for Building Professionals
- Indoor Air Quality

Business Finance
- Business Accounting and Job Cost
- Business Management for Building Professionals
- Construction Contracts and Law
- Estimating
- Finance Banking

Project Management
- Design/Build
- Off-Site Project Management
- On-Site Project Management
- Scheduling

Sales and Marketing
- Customer Service
- Land Development, Site Planning, and Zoning
- Sales and Marketing

Courses (Nine Required)
- Builder Assessment Review (BAR)
- Building Codes and Standards
- Building Technology: Structures and Exterior Finishes
- Building Technology: Systems and Interior Finishes
- Business Accounting and Job Cost
- Business Management for Building Professionals
- Construction Contracts and Law
- Customer Service
- Design/Build
- Energy Efficient Construction
- Estimating
- Finance Banking
- Green Building for Building Professionals
- Indoor Air Quality
- Insurance Reconstruction
- Land Development, Site Planning, and Zoning
- Off-Site Project Management
- On-Site Project Management
- Sales and Marketing
- Scheduling

A further requirement is the completion of twelve hours of continuing education every three years. At least six hours must be from an NAHB University of Housing course.

Certified Graduate Remodeler

An applicant for the Certified Graduate Remodeler (CGR) designation must have a minimum of five years' experience in the remodeling industry, and must complete the Professional Remodelers Experience Profile (PREP) and all courses required by its results.

Results of the PREP determine the number of courses (from no courses to two) in each of the five core areas the candidate is required to complete to obtain the designation:

Marketing and Sales
- Customer Service
- Sales and Marketing for Remodelers

Business Administration
- Business Accounting and Job Cost
- Introduction to Business Management
- Negotiating Skills
- Design, Estimating, and Job Cost
- Design/Build for Remodelers
- Estimating for Builders and Remodelers
- Quality Construction

Contracts, Liability, and Risk Management
- Construction Contracts and Law
- Negotiating Skills
- Risk Management and Insurance for Building Professionals

Project Management
- Off-Site Project Management
- On-Site Project Management
- Scheduling

A further requirement is the completion of twelve hours of continuing education every three years. Six hours must be earned by completing an NAHB University of Housing course that is at least six hours. The remaining six hours may be earned by completing an additional NAHB University of Housing course, taking state or local seminars, NAHB national seminars, or college courses related to the building industry. The continuing education requirement may be completed by either attending or teaching the required education.

Graduate Master Builder

To be eligible for the Graduate Master Builder (GMB) designation, candidates must have previously attained the CGA, CGB, or CGR designation and have five years of building industry experience, or candidates must have completed three CGA, CGB, or CGR courses and have ten years of building industry experience.

Required courses include the following. Five of the six can be waived for holders of CGA, CGB, or CGR designation. Candidates may substitute two CGB-approved courses for any one GMB-approved course, provided those courses were not used to obtain their original CGA, CGB, or CGR designation.

- Diversification: New Profits for Builders
- Financial Management

- Land Acquisition and Development Finance
- Negotiating Skills
- Quality Construction
- Risk Management and Insurance for Building Professionals

A further requirement is the completion of twelve hours of continuing education every three years. At least six hours must be from an NAHB University of Housing course.

Certified Aging-in-Place Specialist

This new designation program teaches the technical, business management, and customer service skills required to meet the needs of the aging-in-place, senior citizens who wish to remodel homes to suit their changing needs.

The program consists of three courses:

- Working with and Marketing to Older Adults
- Home Modifications
- Introduction to Business Management

A further requirement for achieving this designation is attending continuing education programs and/or participating in community service every three years.

Thousands of builders and remodelers have benefited from Home Builders Institute's continuing education programs, sponsored by National Association of Home Builders local home builder associations. To find courses in your area and to learn about fees associated with continuing education programs, visit the NAHB's website at www.nahb.org.

National Association for Women in Construction

The National Association for Women in Construction (NAWIC) Education Foundation offers four opportunities for education and certification through Clemson University. A description of the course work for each follows.

Introduction to Construction

This course introduces the fundamentals of construction processes, procedures, and technology. The specific areas covered include the following:

- City planning
- Regional planning
- Construction management
- Contracting
- Labor and management relations
- Surveying and mapping
- Designing
- Engineering
- Construction materials
- Construction drawings and specifications
- Estimating and bidding
- Scheduling
- Purchasing
- Foundations
- Structures
- Utilities

Certified Industry Technician

This is a self-paced, home-study program. Passing an exam at the end of the course establishes mastery of the material, and upon successful completion of the program, participants will receive the Construction Industry Technician certification, which acknowledges the attainment of a higher professional level in the industry. The curriculum covers:

- Types of construction
- Construction trade associations
- Forms of business ownerships
- Contractual arrangements and contract agreements
- Construction contract documents
- The construction process
- Construction insurance and bonding

Certified Document Specialist

Intended for the intermediate student in construction, this is a textbook course that deals with interpreting information conveyed from the architect/engineer to the contractor by way of a legal document and with implementing that fundamental understanding. It covers the components of the legal agreement that binds the parties in a construction project: working drawings, front-end documents of the project manual, specifications, estimates, proposals, and schedules. It provides a comprehensive understanding of the project's construction documents as needed to prepare an estimate for submitting a bid and to prepare a project schedule for controlling costs after the contract is awarded. Participants must pass an examination to receive the CDS certification.

Certified Construction Associate

This program covers the following areas:

- Business analysis
- Construction environs
- Construction principles
- Effective communication
- Labor relations
- Management techniques

Visit www.nawiceducation.org for more complete information.

Union Education

Many trade unions offer educational and training opportunities for members. In addition to apprenticeships, union members can take advantage of advanced training and specialized courses in areas such as safety or special equipment. Several unions also offer programs in partnership with the Job Corps program.

National Labor College

The National Labor College (NLC) is located in Silver Spring, Maryland. It was founded on the belief of George Meany, longtime president of the AFL-CIO, that labor should have its own educational center to provide resources for union activists.

NLC offers more than seventy weeklong classes in such labor-related areas as arbitration, organizing, negotiation, safety and health, and leadership development. Students can also pursue bachelor's and master's degrees in various disciplines.

The following programs and degrees are offered by NLC:

- Union skills courses
- Building trades courses
- Online and distance education programs
- Southwest organizing school program
- National resource center for OSHA training
- Rail workers HAZMAT training
- Labor safety and health training program
- Bachelor of arts
- Bachelor of technical/professional studies
- Master of arts in legal and ethical studies
- Master's in public administration

For more information about registration and school policies, visit www.nlc.edu.

Other Programs and Partnerships

As the largest contributor to the Home Builders Institute programs, the U.S. Department of Labor has given HBI a $4.2 million grant to increase participation in trades training. "Building Today's Workforce for Tomorrow" funds local and state Home Builder Associations (HBAs) in ten states to develop partnerships with community colleges, K–12 school districts, workforce investment boards, Job Corps centers, and local employers.

HBI's Career Services department provides resources for students, parents, educators, and industry representatives to find career opportunities and sample programs that promote and support partnerships with schools, parents, businesses, and other members of the community. Local home building associations throughout the country have developed industry/education partnership programs that provide middle and high school age students with information about the industry.

Thomson Delmar and HBI partnered to develop the Residential Construction Academy Series of instructional materials. Lowe's Companies Inc. has contributed $150,000 to HBI to establish and maintain the HBI/Lowe's Building Careers Scholarship Fund, which helps the institute's Job Corps graduates make successful transitions to full-time employment in the housing industry.

In partnership with Beazer Homes and Latinos on the Fast Track (LOFT), an initiative of the Hispanic Heritage Foundation and the Hispanic College Fund, HBI has established the Team Builders, the first project of its kind designed to introduce Hispanic youth to careers in residential construction.

In 2005 HBI opened its newest Project TRADE facility in Ocala, Florida. The training site is operated in partnership with nationwide drug and alcohol treatment center Phoenix House and will train students to fill the ten thousand home building vacancies throughout Florida.

3

CARPENTRY AND
RELATED TRADES

CARPENTRY IS CONSIDERED to be the backbone of the construction industry. Because it is such a large component of building construction, we will consider carpentry and its related trades in this chapter.

Carpenters

Carpenters are involved in nearly every type of construction activity, from building highways and bridges to installing kitchen cabinets. Depending on the type of work and the employer, they may specialize in one or two activities or may be required to know how to perform many different tasks. For example, carpenters who work for small home builders and remodeling companies must learn about all aspects of building a house, such as framing walls and partitions, putting in doors and windows, building stairs, installing cabinets and molding, and many other tasks. On the other hand, those who work for large construction contractors or specialty contractors may be required to perform only a few regular tasks, such as framing walls, constructing wooden forms for pouring concrete, or erecting scaffolding. Carpenters also build tunnel bracing, or brattices, in underground passageways and mines to control the circulation of air through the passageways and to work sites.

Although each carpentry task is somewhat different, most involve the same basic steps. Working from blueprints or instructions from supervisors, carpenters first do the layout, which involves measuring, marking, and arranging materials, in accordance with local building codes. They cut and shape wood, plastic, fiberglass, or drywall using hand and power tools such as chisels, planes, saws, drills, and sanders. They then join the materials with nails, screws, staples, or adhesives. In the final step, they check the accuracy of their work with levels, rules, plumb bobs, framing squares, or the electronic versions of these tools, and make any necessary adjustments. The carpenter's job is somewhat easier when working with prefabricated components such as stairs or wall panels because these require less layout work, cutting, and assembly.

Carpenters who work in remodeling need a broad range of skills to perform the many different tasks these jobs may require. Since they are so well trained, these carpenters often can switch from residential building to commercial construction or remodeling work, depending on which offers the best opportunities.

Training Required

Although carpenters can learn their trade through both formal and informal training programs, becoming a skilled carpenter usually takes between three and four years of both classroom and on-the-job training. Although there are a number of different ways to obtain training, in general, a more formal training program will give you better skills and make you more in demand by employers.

You may begin your training in high school, taking classes in English, algebra, geometry, physics, mechanical drawing, blueprint reading, and general shop. After high school, you have a number of different options. You might find a job with a contractor who will provide on-the-job training, where you'll start as a helper or laborer, assisting more experienced workers. During this time, you may elect to attend a trade or vocational school or community college to receive further trade-related training.

Some employers, particularly large nonresidential construction contractors with union membership, offer employees formal apprenticeships that combine on-the-job training with related classroom instruction. To apply for an apprenticeship, you must be at least seventeen years old and meet local requirements; some union locals, for example, test an applicant's aptitude for carpentry. Apprenticeship programs usually last from three to four years, but this may vary depending on your skill.

The United Brotherhood of Carpenters and Joiners of America offers apprenticeship programs throughout the United States and Canada. The carpenter's apprenticeship program is detailed in Chapter 2, under "Apprenticeship Programs." Additional U.S. opportunities are offered by Associated General Contractors Inc. and the Association of Builders and Contractors. All Canadian provinces offer apprenticeship opportunities and participate in the Interprovincial Red Seal program, which was established to provide greater mobility across Canada for skilled workers. Through the program, apprentices who have completed their training and become certified journeymen are able to obtain the Red Seal endorsement on their certificate of qualification by successfully completing an interprovincial examination. This allows them to practice their trade in any province or territory without having to write further examinations.

As an apprentice carpenter, the skills you will learn on the job include structural design, layout, form building, rough framing, and outside and inside finishing. You'll also learn to use the tools, machines, equipment, and materials of the trade. In the classroom, you will receive instruction in safety, first aid, blueprint reading, freehand sketching, basic mathematics, and various carpentry techniques. Both in the classroom and on the job, you'll learn the relationship between carpentry and the other building trades.

Another option is to finish your classroom training before looking for a job. There are a number of public and private vocational-technical schools and training academies affiliated with the unions and contractors that offer training in carpentry, and employers often look favorably upon these students and usually start them at a higher level than those without the training.

The skills you'll need to become a carpenter include manual dexterity, eye-hand coordination, physical fitness, and a good sense of balance. The ability to solve arithmetic problems quickly and accurately also is required. Most contractors also look favorably on a good work history or military service.

Advancement

Because carpenters are exposed to the entire construction process, they usually have greater opportunities than most other construction workers to become general construction supervisors. If you would like to advance, it's increasingly important to be able to communicate in both English and Spanish to relay instructions and safety precautions to workers with limited understanding of English; Spanish-speaking workers make up a large part of the construction workforce in many areas.

Carpenters may advance to positions as carpentry supervisor or general construction supervisor. Many become independent contractors. Both supervisors and contractors need good communication skills to deal with clients and subcontractors, should be able to identify and estimate the quantity of materials needed to complete a job, and should be able to accurately estimate how long a job will take to complete and at what cost.

Compensation

Hourly wage rates for apprentices usually start at about 50 percent of the journeyman rate and increase by about 5 percent in each six-month period until a rate of 85 to 90 percent is reached during the last period of apprenticeship.

In 2004, median hourly earnings of carpenters were $16.78. The majority earned between $12.91 and $22.62, while the lowest 10 percent earned less than $10.36, and the highest 10 percent earned more than $28.65.

Median earnings in the industries employing the largest numbers of carpenters were: nonresidential building construction, $18.70; building finishing contractors, $17.51; residential building construction, $16.48; foundation, structure, and building exterior contractors, $16.40; and employment services, $13.94.

In Canada, median salaries for carpenters in 2004 ranged from $21.00 to $23.00, depending on the location. High salaries were between $27.00 and $30.00; the lowest ranged from $11.00 to $13.00.

Earnings can be reduced on occasion, because carpenters lose work time in bad weather and during recessions when jobs are unavailable. Many carpenters in the United States and Canada are members of the United Brotherhood of Carpenters and Joiners of America (UBC). Member benefits include retirement plans, health insurance, and greater job security.

Job Outlook

Carpentry is the largest construction trade, with more than 1.3 million workers in 2005; about one-third were self-employed. Despite current slowdowns, job opportunities over the next ten years should be excellent because high turnover rates create many openings.

The best opportunities will be for carpenters with the most skills. Contractors report having trouble finding skilled carpenters to fill many of their openings, due in part to the fact that many people with limited skills take jobs as carpenters but eventually leave the occupation because they dislike the work or cannot find steady employment.

The need for carpenters is expected to grow as construction activity increases in response to demand for new housing and office and retail space and for modernizing and expanding schools and industrial plants. A strong home remodeling market will also contribute to the demand.

However, some of this demand will be offset by increased productivity resulting from the growing use of prefabricated components and improved fasteners and tools. Prefabricated wall panels, roof assemblies and stairs, and pre-hung doors and windows can be installed very quickly; instead of having to be built on the work site, they can be lifted into place in one operation. New and improved tools, equipment, techniques, and materials also have vastly increased carpenters' versatility.

Carpenters with all-round skills will have better opportunities for steady work than those who can perform only a few relatively simple, routine tasks. Periods of unemployment do occur because of the short-term nature of many construction projects, winter slowdowns in construction activity in northern areas, and the cyclical nature of the construction industry.

Job opportunities for carpenters also vary by geographic area. Construction activity parallels the movement of people and businesses and reflects differences in local economic conditions. The areas with the largest population increases will also provide the best job opportunities for carpenters and apprenticeship opportunities for persons seeking to enter carpentry.

Insulation Workers

We all want our homes to be warm in winter and cool in the summer. To achieve this, our homes and working environments must be properly insulated to reduce energy consumption. Refrigerated storage rooms, vats, tanks, vessels, boilers, and steam and hot-water pipes also are insulated to prevent the wasteful loss of heat.

Insulation workers install the materials used to insulate buildings and equipment by cementing, stapling, wiring, taping, or spraying insulation. They cover steam pipes by measuring and cutting sections of insulation to the proper length, slipping it over the pipe, and fastening it with adhesive, staples, tape, or wire bands. To cover a wall or other flat surface, they use a hose to spray foam insulation onto a wire mesh that provides a rough surface to which the foam can cling and that adds strength to the finished surface. They may then install drywall or apply a final coat of plaster for a finished appearance. In attics or exterior walls of uninsulated buildings, workers may blow in loose-fill insulation. A helper feeds a machine with fiberglass, cellulose, or rock-wool insulation, while another worker blows the insulation with a compressor hose into the space being filled.

In new construction or on major renovations, insulation workers staple fiberglass or rock-wool batts to exterior walls and ceilings before drywall, paneling, or plaster walls are put in place. In major renovations, they often must first remove the old insulation. In the past, asbestos was used extensively in walls and ceilings and to cover pipes, boilers, and industrial equipment, but it has since been found to cause cancer in humans. Because of this danger, both the U.S. Environmental Protection Agency and Environment Canada require that asbestos be removed before a building undergoes major renovations or is demolished. This work is performed by specially trained workers who remove the asbestos before insulation workers can install the new insulating materials. The work of these specialists is profiled in Chapter 8.

Insulation workers use common hand tools, such as trowels, brushes, knives, scissors, saws, pliers, and stapling guns. They may use power saws to cut insulating materials, welding machines to join sheet metal or secure clamps, and compressors to blow or spray insulation.

Training Required

Most insulation workers learn their trade informally on the job, although some complete formal apprenticeship programs. For entry-level jobs, contractors prefer high school graduates who are in good physical condition and licensed to drive. High school courses in blueprint reading, shop, mathematics, science, sheet metal layout, woodworking, and general construction will provide you with a good background. You should be at least eighteen years old and have a high school diploma to apply for an apprenticeship.

If you choose to learn the trade on the job, you'll receive instruction and supervision from experienced insulation workers. You'll start with simple tasks, such as carrying insulation or holding material while it is fastened in place. On-the-job training can take up to two years, depending on the nature of the work—installing insulation in homes generally requires less training than learning to apply it in commercial and industrial settings. As you gain experience, you will receive less supervision, more responsibility, and higher pay. A certification program has been developed by insulation contractor organizations to help all workers prove their skills and knowledge. You'll need at least six months of experience before you can complete certification. Certification is currently limited to residential installation; it is also currently under development for industrial settings.

In-depth instruction in all phases of insulation is provided by apprenticeship programs, which are offered by a joint committee of local insulation contractors and the local union of the International Association of Heat and Frost Insulators and Asbestos Workers. Programs normally consist of four years of on-the-job training coupled with classroom instruction, and trainees must pass practical and written tests to demonstrate their knowledge of the trade.

Advancement

Skilled insulation workers may advance to supervisor, shop superintendent, or insulation contract estimator, or they may set up their own insulation business.

Compensation

Median hourly earnings in 2004 of floor, ceiling, and wall insulation workers were $14.57. The middle 50 percent earned between $10.63 and $20.20, while the lowest 10 percent earned less than $8.53, and the highest 10 percent earned more than $27.35. Median hourly earnings of mechanical insulation workers were $16.03, with most earning between $12.16 and $21.15.

Median hourly earnings in the industries employing the largest numbers of insulation workers were: insulation workers and mechanical-equipment contractors, $15.66; building finishing contractors, $15.55; insulation workers and floor, ceiling, and wall finishing contractors, $13.95.

Union workers generally earn more than nonunion workers. Apprentices start at about half the journeyman's wages. Insulation workers doing commercial and industrial work earn substantially more than those working in residential construction, which does not require as much skill.

Job Outlook

Job opportunities are expected to be good in this trade. Because there are no strict training requirements for entry, many people with limited skills work as insulation workers for a short time and then move on to other types of work, creating many job openings. In addition, openings will arise from the need to replace workers who retire or leave the labor force for other reasons.

In contrast to other construction trades, insulation workers work mainly on new construction, which is expected to moderate somewhat over the next decade. Although the increased efficiency of installation techniques—such as blow-in and spray-in insulation, which allows more work to be done in a shorter period of time and with fewer people—may limit growth somewhat, some demand will be spurred by the continuing need for energy-efficient buildings, which will generate work in existing structures as well as in new construction.

There may be periods of unemployment because of the short duration of many construction projects and the cyclical nature of construction activity. Workers employed to perform industrial plant maintenance generally have more stable employment because maintenance and repair must be done on a continuing basis. Most insulation is applied after buildings are enclosed, so weather conditions have less effect on the employment of insulation workers than on that of some other construction occupations.

Drywall and Ceiling Tile Installers and Tapers

Most people don't think about what their walls and ceilings are made of. We take for granted that they've been installed properly and will last perhaps forever. But your interest in building makes you want to know just what's behind the paint and wallpaper you see every day.

Drywall consists of a thin layer of gypsum between two layers of heavy paper. It is used to construct walls and ceilings in most buildings today because it's both faster and cheaper to install than plaster. Although drywall is commonly called *sheetrock*, the term *Sheetrock* is actually the registered brand name of the most commonly used drywall product.

Drywall workers fall into two categories—installers and tapers—but many do both types of work. Installers, also called *applicators* or *hangers*, fasten drywall panels to the inside framework of buildings. *Tapers*, or *finishers*, prepare these panels for painting by taping and finishing joints and imperfections.

Because drywall panels are manufactured in standard sizes (usually four feet by eight or twelve feet), installers must measure, cut, and fit some pieces around doors and windows. They also saw or cut holes in panels for electrical outlets, air-conditioning units, and plumbing. After making these alterations, they glue, nail, or screw the wallboard panels to the wood or metal framework. Because drywall is heavy and cumbersome, a helper generally assists the installer in positioning and securing the panel. Workers often use a lift when placing ceiling panels.

After the drywall is installed, tapers fill joints between panels with a joint compound. Using the wide, flat tip of a special trowel, they spread the compound into and along each side of the joint with brushlike strokes and immediately use the trowel to press a paper tape that reinforces the drywall and hides imperfections into the wet compound and smooth away excess material. Nail and screw depressions also are covered with this compound, as are imperfections caused by the installation of air-conditioning vents and other fixtures. On large projects, finishers may use automatic taping tools that apply the joint compound and tape in one step. Tapers apply second and third coats of the compound, sanding the treated areas where needed after each coat to make them as smooth as the rest of the wall surface. This results in a very smooth and almost perfect surface. Some tapers apply textured surfaces to walls and ceilings with trowels, brushes, or spray guns.

Ceiling tile installers, or acoustical carpenters, apply or mount acoustical tiles or blocks, strips, or sheets of shock-absorbing materials to ceilings and walls of buildings to reduce reflection of sound or to decorate rooms. First, they measure and mark the surface according to blueprints and drawings. Then, they nail or screw moldings to the wall to support and seal the joint between the ceiling tile and the wall. Finally, they mount the tile, either by applying a cement adhesive to the back of the tile and then pressing the tile into place or by nailing, screwing, stapling, or wire-tying the lath directly to the structural framework.

This occupation also includes *lathers*, who fasten metal or rockboard lath to walls, ceilings, and partitions of buildings. Lath forms the support base for plaster, fireproofing, or acoustical materials. At one time, lath was made of wooden strips, but today lathers work mostly with wire, metal mesh, or rockboard lath. Using hand tools and portable power tools, lathers nail, screw, staple, or wire-tie the lath directly to the structural framework.

Training Required

You can learn drywall and ceiling tile installation and taping through both formal and informal training programs. Although between three and four years of both classroom and on-the-job training may be required to become skilled, many of the required skills can be learned within the first year.

There are a number of different training options you can choose. The most common is to find a job with a contractor who will provide on-the-job training. You'll start as a helper, assisting more experienced workers, and may also take courses at a trade or vocational school or at a community college.

Some employers offer formal apprenticeships that combine on-the-job training with related classroom instruction. In most cases, you must be at least eighteen years old and meet local requirements to enter into an apprenticeship. The length of the program, usually three to four years, will vary depending on your skill level. However, because the number of apprenticeship programs is limited, only a small proportion of workers learn their trade through these programs.

You also have the option to complete your classroom training before seeking a job. There are a number of both public and private vocational-technical schools and training academies affiliated with the unions and contractors that offer training, and many employers prefer applicants who have attended these programs over those without the training.

As an entry-level installer helper, you'll start by carrying materials, lifting and holding panels, and cleaning up debris. You will also learn to use the tools, machines, equipment, and materials of the trade. Within a few weeks, you'll learn to measure, cut, and install materials and will eventually become a fully experienced worker. If you focus on taping, you'll learn the job by taping joints and touching up nail holes, scrapes, and other imperfections and then move on to installing corner guards and concealing openings around pipes. At the end of your training, you will learn to estimate the cost of installing and finishing drywall.

If you decide to start your training in high school, you should take classes in English, math, mechanical drawing, blueprint reading, and general shop. You will also need good manual dexterity, good eye-hand coordination, good physical fitness, a good sense of balance, and the ability to solve arithmetic problems quickly and accurately.

Advancement

Workers in this trade may advance to carpentry supervisor or general construction supervisor positions; others may become independent contractors. The ability to communicate in both English and Spanish is increasingly important for advancement because of the increasing number of Spanish-speaking workers in the construction industry. Hispanic workers who want to advance should learn English. Supervisors and contractors need good English skills to deal with clients and subcontractors. They also should be able to identify and estimate the quantity of materials needed to complete a job and accurately estimate how long a job will take to complete and at what cost.

Compensation

In 2004, the median hourly earnings of drywall and ceiling tile installers were $16.36. Most earned between $12.59 and $21.82, while the lowest paid earned less than $9.98, and the highest more than $28.30. The median hourly earnings in the industries that employed the largest numbers of these workers were: residential building construction, $17.33; building finishing contractors, $16.53; and nonresidential building construction, $14.57.

The median hourly earnings of tapers were $18.78. While the majority earned between $14.07 and $24.43, the lowest 10 percent earned less than $10.66, and the highest 10 percent earned more than $28.79.

Some contractors pay these workers according to the number of panels they install or finish per day; others pay an hourly rate. A forty-hour week is standard, but the workweek may sometimes be longer or shorter. Workers who are paid hourly rates receive premium pay for overtime. Trainees usually start at about half the rate paid to experienced workers and receive wage increases as they became more highly skilled.

Job Outlook

Job opportunities in this trade are expected to be good, especially for those with the most experience. In addition to jobs involving traditional interior work, drywall workers will find employment opportunities in the installation of insulated exterior wall systems, which are becoming increasingly popular.

Some drywall installers, ceiling tile installers, and tapers with limited skills leave the occupation when they find that they dislike the work or fail to find steady employment, which will lead to many additional jobs each year.

Despite the growing use of exterior panels, most drywall installation and finishing is done indoors. Therefore, drywall workers lose less work time because of inclement weather than do some other construction workers. Nevertheless, they may be unemployed between construction projects and during downturns in construction activity.

Plasterers and Stucco Masons

Plastering is one of the oldest crafts in the building trades, and it remains popular due to the relatively low cost of the material and overall durability of work. The ancient Egyptians used plaster, and the Romans employed it for walls and ceilings and in sculpture. Today, the potential uses for plaster are constantly expanding as new products and systems are introduced.

Plasterers apply plaster to interior walls and ceilings to form fire-resistant and relatively soundproof surfaces. They also apply plaster veneer over drywall to create smooth or textured abrasion-resistant finishes. In addition, they install prefabricated exterior insulation systems over existing walls for good insulation and interesting architectural effects, and they cast ornamental designs in plaster.

Stucco masons apply durable plasters, such as polymer-based acrylic finishes and stucco, to exterior surfaces.

Plasterers can plaster either solid surfaces, such as concrete block, or supportive wire mesh—the lath. When working with such interior surfaces as concrete block, they first apply a brown coat of gypsum plaster that provides a base, which is followed by a second, or finish, coat (also called *white coat*) made of a lime-based plaster. When plastering metal lath foundations, they apply a preparatory, or *scratch*, coat with a trowel, spreading this rich plaster mixture into and over the metal lath. Before the plaster sets, they scratch its surface with a rakelike tool to produce ridges, so that the subsequent brown coat will bond tightly.

Helpers prepare a thick, smooth plaster for the brown coat. Plasterers spray or trowel this mixture onto the surface, then finish by smoothing it to an even, level surface.

For the finish coat, plasterers prepare a mixture of lime, plaster of paris, and water, which they quickly apply to the brown coat using a *hawk*, which is a light, metal plate with a handle, trowel, brush, and water. This mixture, which sets quickly, produces a very smooth, durable finish.

Plasterers also work with a material that can be finished in a single coat. This thin-coat, or gypsum veneer plaster, is made of lime and plaster of paris and is mixed with water at the job site. It provides a smooth, durable, abrasion-resistant finish on interior masonry surfaces, special gypsum baseboard, or drywall prepared with a bonding agent.

They create decorative interior surfaces as well. One way that they do this is by pressing a brush or trowel firmly against a wet plaster surface and using a circular hand motion to create decorative swirls.

For exterior work, stucco masons usually apply stucco, which is a mixture of portland cement, lime, and sand, over cement, concrete, masonry, or lath. It may also be applied directly to a wire lath with a scratch coat, followed by a brown coat and then a finish coat. Stucco masons may also embed marble or gravel chips into the finish coat to achieve a pebblelike, decorative finish.

When required, plasterers apply insulation to the exteriors of both new and old buildings. They cover the outer wall with rigid foam insulation board and reinforcing mesh and then trowel on a polymer-based or polymer-modified base coat. They may apply an additional coat of this material with a decorative finish.

Plasterers sometimes do complex decorative and ornamental work that requires special skill and creativity. For example, they may mold intricate wall and ceiling designs. Following an architect's blueprint, they pour or spray a special plaster into a mold and allow it to set. Workers then remove the molded plaster and put it in place, according to the plan.

Training Required

You can take a formal or informal route to learn this trade. If you choose to learn informally, you'll start as a helper for experienced workers. You may need between two and three years of on-the-job training supplemented by formal classroom training to become a skilled plasterer or stucco mason.

You can start preparing in high school by taking classes in mathematics, mechanical drawing, and general shop. After high school, you have a number of different training options. The most common is to find a job with a contractor who will provide on-the-job training, where you'll start as a helper, assisting more experienced workers by carrying materials, setting up scaffolds, and mixing plaster. Later, you'll learn to apply the scratch, brown, and finish coats and may also learn to replicate plaster decorations for restoration work. In some cases, your employer may enroll you in an employer-provided training program or send you to a trade or vocational school or community college to receive further classroom training.

Although most employers recommend apprenticeship as the best way to learn plastering, apprenticeships for this occupation are few. Apprenticeship programs are sponsored by local joint committees of contractors and unions and generally consist of two or three years of on-the-job training, in addition to at least 144 hours annually of classroom instruction in drafting, blueprint reading, and mathematics for layout work.

In the classroom, you'll learn the history of the trade and the industry, as well as the uses of plaster, estimating materials and costs, and casting ornamental plaster designs. On the job, you'll learn about lath bases, plaster mixes, methods of plastering, blueprint reading, and safety. You will also learn how to use various tools, such as hand and powered trowels, floats, brushes, straightedges, power tools, plaster-mixing machines, and piston-type pumps. Some apprenticeship programs allow you to obtain training in related occupations, such as cement masonry and bricklaying.

To apply for a job as apprentice or helper, you must be at least eighteen years old, be in good physical condition, and have good manual dexterity. Most employers prefer that you have a high school education. Courses in general mathematics, mechanical drawing, and shop provide a useful background.

Advancement

With additional training and experience, plasterers and stucco masons may advance to positions as supervisors, superintendents, or estimators for plastering contractors. Many become self-employed contractors. Others become building inspectors.

Compensation

In 2004, median hourly earnings of plasterers and stucco masons were $15.60. Most earned between $12.27 and $20.32. The lowest 10 percent earned less than $9.80, and the highest earned more than $26.84.

The median hourly earnings in the largest industries employing plasterers and stucco masons were $15.75 for building finishing contractors and $14.62 for foundation, structure, and building exterior contractors.

Apprentice wage rates start at about half the rate paid to experienced plasterers and stucco masons. Annual earnings for plasterers and stucco masons and apprentices can be less than the hourly rate would indicate, because poor weather and periodic declines in construction activity can limit work hours.

Job Outlook

Job opportunities for plasterers and stucco masons are expected to be good through 2014. Most openings will be the result of plasterers and stucco masons transferring to other occupations or leaving the labor force. The best employment opportunities should continue to be in Florida, California, and the Southwest, where exterior plaster and decorative finishes are expected to remain popular. Plastering in the Northeast continues to remain in demand, especially in restoration.

In past years, employment of plasterers declined as more builders switched to drywall construction. However, this decline has halted, and employment of plasterers is expected to grow as a result of the appreciation for the durability and attractiveness that troweled finishes provide. Thin-coat plastering, or veneering, in particular is gaining wide acceptance as more builders recognize its ease of application, durability, quality of finish, and soundproofing and fire-retarding qualities, although the increased use of fire sprinklers will reduce the demand for fire-resistant plasterwork. Prefabricated wall systems and new polymer-based or polymer-modified acrylic exterior insulating finishes also are gaining popularity, particularly in the South and Southwest regions of the country. This is not only because of their durability, attractiveness, and insulating properties, but also because of their relatively low cost. In addition, plasterers will be needed to renovate plasterwork in old structures and to create special architectural effects, such as curved surfaces, which are not practical with drywall materials.

Most plasterers and stucco masons work in construction, where prospects fluctuate from year to year due to changing economic conditions. Bad weather affects plastering less than other construction trades because most work is indoors. However, on exterior surfacing jobs, plasterers and stucco masons may lose time because plastering materials cannot be applied under wet or freezing conditions.

A Final Word

You've seen in this chapter that although many people automatically think of carpenters when they consider building construction careers, there are indeed many other options in related trades. If you consider your skills and interests and the degree of training you wish to pursue, you should be able to find a trade that will serve you well throughout your career.

4

Exterior Trades

Apart from the actual construction, several other trades are involved in a building project. Some work primarily on the exterior of the building, while others work indoors.

Most building projects require site preparation, walkways, secure roofs, and perhaps even roads. The following trades are those involved in doing this exterior work.

Construction Equipment Operators

Before any actual construction can begin, the site has to be prepared for the project, whether it is a residential home, office building, industrial plant, or highway. This work is done by construction equipment operators, who use machinery to move construction materials, earth, and other heavy materials at construction sites, mines, and sometimes your backyard. Also called *operating engineers*, these workers operate equipment that clears and grades land to prepare it for the construction of roads, buildings, and neighborhoods. They dig trenches to lay or repair sewers and other pipelines, and they hoist heavy construction materials. They may even work offshore constructing oil rigs. They also operate machinery that applies asphalt and concrete to roads and other structures.

Operators control equipment by moving levers or foot pedals, operating switches, or turning dials. The operation of much of this equipment is becoming more complex as a result of computerized controls. Global Positioning System (GPS) technology also is being used to help with grading and leveling activities. In addition to controlling the equipment, operators set up and inspect the equipment, make adjustments, and perform some maintenance and minor repairs.

This trade includes the following categories: operating engineers and other construction equipment operators; paving, surfacing, and tamping equipment operators; and pile-driver operators. Operating engineers and other construction equipment operators run one or several types of power construction equipment. They may operate excavation and loading machines equipped with scoops, shovels, or buckets that dig sand, gravel, earth, or similar materials and load it into trucks or onto conveyors. In addition to the familiar bulldozers, they operate trench excavators, road graders, and similar equipment. Some drive and control industrial trucks or tractors equipped with forklifts or booms for lifting materials or with hitches for pulling trailers. They also operate and maintain air compressors, pumps, and other power equipment at construction sites. Construction equipment operators classified as operating engineers are capable of operating several different types of construction equipment.

Paving and surfacing equipment operators use levers and other controls to operate machines that spread and level asphalt or spread and smooth concrete for roadways or other structures. Asphalt paving machine operators turn valves to regulate the temperature and flow of asphalt onto the roadbed. They must take care that the machine distributes the paving material evenly and without voids and make sure that there is a constant flow of asphalt going into the hopper. Concrete paving machine operators control levers and turn handwheels to move attachments that spread, vibrate, and level wet concrete within forms. They must observe the surface of concrete to identify low spots into which workers must add concrete. They use other attachments to smooth the surface of the concrete, spray on a curing compound, and cut expansion joints. Tamping equipment operators operate machines that compact earth and other fill materials for roadbeds. They also may operate machines with interchangeable hammers to cut or break up old pavement and drive guardrail posts into the earth.

Pile-driver operators control large machines—mounted on skids, barges, or cranes—that hammer piles into the ground. Piles are long heavy beams of wood or steel driven into the ground to support retaining walls, bulkheads, bridges, piers, or building foundations. Some work on offshore oil rigs. Pile-driver operators move hand-and-foot levers and turn valves to activate, position, and control the pile-driving equipment.

Training Required

Most operating engineers learn their skills on the job, starting by operating light equipment under the guidance of an experienced worker. Later, they may operate heavier equipment, such as bull-dozers and cranes. However, you will gain more comprehensive skills through formal training. You may choose to take part in a formal apprenticeship program administered by union-management committees of the International Union of Operating Engineers and the Associated General Contractors of America. As an apprentice, you'll learn to operate a wider variety of machines than other beginners, which will likely lead to better job opportunities. Apprenticeship programs consist of at least three years, or six thousand hours, of on-the-job training and 144 hours a year of related classroom instruction.

Most employers generally prefer to hire high school graduates, although some may train nongraduates to operate some types of equipment. Technologically advanced construction equipment has computerized controls and improved hydraulics and electronics that require more skill to operate, so you may need more training and some understanding of electronics to operate this equipment. Mechanical aptitude and high school training in automobile mechanics are helpful because your work may include performing some maintenance on the machines. High school courses in science and mechanical drawing and experience operating related mobile equipment, such as farm tractors or heavy equipment, are also assets.

Private vocational schools offer instruction in the operation of certain types of construction equipment. Completion of such a program may help you to find a job as a trainee or apprentice, but you should check the school's reputation among employers in the area and find out if it offers the opportunity to work on actual machines in realistic situations.

To operate construction equipment, you need to be in good physical condition and have a good sense of balance, the ability to judge distance, and eye-hand-foot coordination. Some operator positions require the ability to work at heights.

Compensation

Earnings in this field vary. In 2004, median hourly earnings of operating engineers and other construction equipment operators were $17.00. Most earned between $13.19 and $23.00. Median hourly earnings of paving, surfacing, and tamping equipment operators were $14.42 in 2004, with most earning between $11.35 and $19.30. Median hourly earnings of pile-driver operators were $21.29. The majority earned between $15.50 and $30.23.

Pay scales generally are higher in large metropolitan areas than elsewhere. Annual earnings of some workers may be lower than hourly rates would indicate because work time may be limited by bad weather.

Job Outlook

Job opportunities for construction equipment operators are expected to be good through 2014, even as improvements in equipment should continue to raise worker productivity and, therefore, moderate demand for these workers. Employment is expected to increase as population and business growth create a need for new houses, industrial facilities, schools, hospitals, offices, and other structures. More construction equipment operators also will be needed as a result of expected growth in highway, bridge, and street construction. Bridge construction is expected to grow the fastest because of the need to repair or replace structures before they become unsafe. Highway conditions also will spur demand for highway maintenance and repair. In addition to job growth, many job openings will arise because of the need to replace experienced construction equipment operators who transfer to other occupations, retire, or leave the job for other reasons.

Like that of other construction workers, employment of construction equipment operators is sensitive to fluctuations in the economy. Workers may experience periods of unemployment when the level of construction activity falls.

Structural and Reinforcing Iron and Metal Workers

If you've ever wondered what makes a building or bridge stay up, it's the structural and reinforcing iron and steel that form the basis on which the other trades can work.

Structural and reinforcing iron and metal workers place and install iron or steel girders, columns, and other construction materials to form buildings, bridges, and other structures. They also position and secure steel bars or mesh in concrete forms to reinforce the concrete used in highways, buildings, bridges, and tunnels. In addition, they repair and renovate older buildings and structures. Even though the primary metal involved in this work is steel, they are often called *ironworkers*. Some ironworkers fabricate structural metal in fabricating shops, which are usually located away from the construction site.

Before construction can begin, ironworkers must erect steel frames and assemble the cranes and derricks that move structural steel, reinforcing bars, buckets of concrete, lumber, and other materials and equipment around the construction site. Once this job has been completed, workers begin to connect steel columns, beams, and girders according to blueprints and instructions from supervisors and superintendents. Structural steel, reinforcing rods, and ornamental iron generally come to the construction site ready for erection, cut to the proper size, with holes drilled for bolts, and numbered for assembly.

Ironworkers at the construction site unload and stack the prefabricated steel so that it can be hoisted easily when needed. To do this, they attach cables (slings) to the steel and to the crane or derrick. One worker directs the hoist operator with hand signals while another holds a rope (tag line) attached to the steel to prevent it from swinging. The crane or derrick hoists steel into place in the framework, where two connectors position it with connecting bars and spud wrenches (a long wrench with a pointed handle). Workers using drift pins or the handle of a spud wrench align the holes in the steel with the holes in the framework. Before the bolts are permanently tightened, ironworkers check vertical and horizontal alignment with plumb bobs, laser equipment, transits, or levels; then they bolt or weld the piece permanently in place.

Reinforcing iron and rebar workers set reinforcing bars (often called *rebar*) in the forms that hold concrete, following blueprints showing the location, size, and number of bars. They then fasten the bars together by tying wire around them with pliers. When reinforcing floors, ironworkers place spacers under the rebar to hold the bars off the deck. Although these materials usually arrive ready to use, workers occasionally must cut bars with metal shears or acetylene torches, bend them by hand or machine, or weld them with arc-welding equipment.

Some concrete is reinforced with welded wire fabric. Using hooked rods, workers cut and fit the fabric, and while a concrete crew places the concrete, ironworkers properly position the fabric into the concrete. Post-tensioning is another technique used in reinforcing concrete. In this technique, workers substitute cables for reinforcing bars. When the concrete is poured, the ends of the cables are left exposed. After the concrete cures, ironworkers tighten the cables with jacking equipment specially designed for the purpose. Post-tensioning allows designers to create larger open areas in a building, because supports can be placed further apart. This technique is commonly employed in parking garages and arenas.

Ornamental ironworkers install stairs, handrails, curtain walls (the nonstructural walls and window frames of many large buildings), and other miscellaneous metal after the structure of the building has been completed. As they hoist pieces into position, ornamental ironworkers make sure that the pieces are properly fitted and aligned before bolting or welding them for a secure fit.

Training Required

Most employers recommend a three- or four-year apprenticeship consisting of on-the-job training and evening classroom instruction as the best way to learn this trade. Apprenticeship programs are administered by committees made up of representatives of local unions of the International Association of Bridge, Structural, Ornamental, and Reinforcing Iron Workers or the local chapters of contractors' associations.

You must be at least eighteen years old to get a job as an ironworker, and most employers and local apprenticeship committees will prefer that you have earned a high school diploma as well. High school courses in general mathematics, mechanical drawing, English, and welding are a good foundation. You must be in good physical condition to handle the heavy and bulky materials used in this trade. In addition, you need good agility, balance, eyesight, and depth perception to work safely at great heights on narrow beams and girders, and you should not be afraid of heights or suffer from dizziness.

In the classroom, you'll study blueprint reading, mathematics, the basics of structural erecting, rigging, reinforcing, welding, assembling, and safety training, as well as the care and safe use of tools and materials. On the job, you'll work in all aspects of the trade, such as unloading and storing materials at the job site, rigging materials for movement by crane, connecting structural steel, and welding.

It is possible to learn ironworking informally on the job, without completing an apprenticeship. If you choose this path, you will most likely not receive classroom training, although some large contractors have extensive training programs. As an on-the-job trainee, you'll begin by assisting experienced ironworkers on simple jobs, such as carrying various materials. With experience, you'll perform more difficult tasks, such as cutting and fitting different parts; however, learning through work experience alone may not provide training as complete as an apprenticeship program, and it usually takes longer.

Advancement

Some experienced workers are promoted to supervisor. Others may go into the contracting business for themselves. The ability to communicate in both English and Spanish will improve opportunities for advancement.

Compensation

In 2004, median hourly earnings of structural iron and steel workers in all industries were $20.40. While most earned between

$14.84 and $27.21, the lowest 10 percent earned less than $11.25, and the highest earned more than $33.53. Median hourly earnings of reinforcing iron and rebar workers in all industries were $16.90. The middle 50 percent earned between $12.45 and $25.94, while the lowest paid earned less than $10.03, and the highest earned more than $32.59.

Median hourly earnings of structural iron and steel workers in 2004 for foundation, structure, and building exterior contractors were $21.81 and in nonresidential building construction, $17.47. Reinforcing iron and rebar workers earned median hourly earnings of $16.52 working for foundation, structure, and building exterior contractors.

About half of the workers in this trade are members of the International Association of Bridge, Structural, Ornamental, and Reinforcing Iron Workers. According to the union, average hourly earnings, including benefits, for structural and reinforcing metal workers who belonged to a union and worked full-time were slightly higher than the hourly earnings of nonunion workers. Structural and reinforcing iron and metal workers in New York, Boston, San Francisco, Chicago, Los Angeles, Philadelphia, and other large cities received the highest wages.

Apprentices generally start at about 50 percent to 60 percent of the rate paid to experienced journeymen. Throughout the course of the apprenticeship program, as they acquire the skills of the trade, they receive periodic increases until their pay approaches that of experienced workers.

Earnings for ironworkers may be reduced on occasion because work can be limited by bad weather, the short-term nature of construction jobs, and economic downturns.

Job Outlook

Employment is expected to grow 9 to 17 percent through the year 2014, largely on the basis of projected growth in nonresidential and heavy construction. The rehabilitation, maintenance, and replacement of a growing number of older buildings, highways, power plants, and bridges are also expected to create employment opportunities. Federal, state, and provincial legislatures continue to support and fund the building of roads, which will secure jobs for the near future. Many job openings will result from the need to replace experienced ironworkers who leave the occupation or retire.

In most areas, job opportunities should be good for those with the best qualifications, although the number of openings can fluctuate from year to year with economic conditions and the level of construction activity. Ironworkers can experience periods of unemployment during economic downturns. Similarly, job opportunities may vary widely by geographic area. Population growth in the South and West should create more job opportunities than elsewhere as buildings and roads are constructed to meet the needs of the people. Job openings for ironworkers usually are more abundant during the spring and summer months, when the level of construction activity increases. Workers who are willing to relocate are often able to find work in other areas.

Cement and Concrete Masons and Terrazzo Workers

The concrete mason provides much of the structure in which we live and work. The cement mason lays the roads on which we travel and the runways from which we fly. He or she can make a solid floor, a driveway, a sidewalk, steps from a house or into a garden, street curbs and gutters, as well as pour cement foundation walls, piers, and whole concrete walls—all with precision and finesse.

Cement is so overwhelmingly important to construction that it would be difficult to replace it with other materials. It has one quality that is, in a sense, unique. It is liquid, and in this state it can be formed into any shape, form, or object. After it hardens it has the quality of a very durable material. Reinforced with steel, it provides the best possible combination of flexibility, durability, and strength.

Cement masons and concrete finishers place and finish the concrete. They also may color concrete surfaces, expose aggregate (small stones) in walls and sidewalks, or fabricate concrete beams, columns, and panels. In preparing a site for placing concrete, masons first set and align the forms for holding the concrete. They then direct the casting of the concrete and supervise laborers who use shovels or special tools to spread it. Masons then guide a straightedge back and forth across the top of the forms to *screed*, or level, the freshly placed concrete. Immediately after leveling the concrete, masons carefully smooth the surface with a *bull float*, a long-handled tool about eight by forty-eight inches that covers the coarser materials in the concrete and brings a rich mixture of fine cement paste to the surface.

After the concrete has been leveled and floated, finishers press an edger between the forms and the concrete and guide it along the edge and the surface to produce slightly rounded edges that help prevent chipping or cracking. Concrete finishers use a special tool called a *groover* to make joints or grooves at specific intervals that help control cracking. Next, they trowel the surface using either a powered or hand trowel, a small, smooth, rectangular metal tool.

Sometimes, cement masons perform all the steps of laying concrete, including the finishing. As the final step, they retrowel the concrete surface back and forth with powered and hand trowels to create a smooth finish. For a coarse, nonskid finish, they brush the surface with a broom or stiff-bristled brush. For a pebble finish, they embed small gravel chips into the surface. They then wash any excess cement from the exposed chips with a mild acid solution. For color, they use colored premixed concrete. On concrete surfaces that will remain exposed after the forms are stripped, such as columns, ceilings, and wall panels, masons cut away high spots and loose concrete with hammer and chisel, fill any large indentations with a portland cement paste, and smooth the surface with a Carborundum stone. Finally, they coat the exposed area with a rich cement mixture, using either a special tool or a coarse cloth to rub the concrete to a uniform finish.

Throughout the entire process, cement masons must monitor how the wind, heat, or cold affects the curing of the concrete. They must have a thorough knowledge of concrete characteristics so that, by using sight and touch, they can determine what is happening to the concrete and take measures to prevent defects.

Segmental pavers lay out, cut, and install pavers, which are flat pieces of masonry usually made from compacted concrete or brick. Pavers are used to pave paths, patios, playgrounds, driveways, and steps. They are manufactured in various textures and often interlock together to form an attractive pattern. Segmental pavers first prepare the site by removing the existing pavement or soil. They grade the remaining soil to the proper depth and determine the amount of base material needed, depending on the local soil conditions. They then install and compact the base material, a granular material that compacts easily, and lay the pavers from the center out, so that any trimmed pieces will be on the outside rather than in the center. Then, they install edging materials to prevent the pavers from shifting and fill the spaces between with dry sand.

Terrazzo workers create attractive walkways, floors, patios, and panels by exposing marble chips and other fine aggregates on the surface of finished concrete. Much of their preliminary work is similar to that of cement masons. Attractive, marble-chip terrazzo requires three layers of materials. First, cement masons or terrazzo workers build a solid, level concrete foundation that is three to four inches deep. After the forms are removed from the foundation, workers add a one-inch layer of sandy concrete, into which they partially embed, or attach with adhesive, metal divider strips wherever there is to be a joint or change of color in the terrazzo. For the final layer, they blend and place into each of the panels a fine marble chip mixture that may be color-pigmented. While the mixture is still wet, workers add additional marble chips of various colors into each panel and roll a lightweight roller over the entire surface.

When the terrazzo is thoroughly set, helpers grind it with a terrazzo grinder, which is somewhat like a floor polisher, only much heavier. Any depressions left by the grinding are filled with a matching grout material and hand-troweled for a smooth, uniform surface. Terrazzo workers then clean, polish, and seal the dry surface for a lustrous finish.

Training Required

Most workers learn their trades either through on-the-job training as helpers or through three-year or four-year apprenticeship programs. Some attend trade or vocational-technical schools.

Working as a construction laborer is an option for learning the trade. Most employers prefer to hire helpers and apprentices who are high school graduates and at least eighteen years old, who possess a driver's license, and who are in good physical condition. The ability to get along with others is also important because cement masons frequently work in teams. High school courses in general science, mathematics, and vocational-technical subjects, such as blueprint reading and mechanical drawing, will provide you with a good background.

You can enroll in an on-the-job training program that consists of informal instruction, in which experienced workers teach you to use the tools, equipment, machines, and materials of the trade. As a trainee, you'll begin with tasks such as edging, jointing, and using a straightedge on freshly placed concrete. As training progresses, assignments will become more complex, and you can usually do finishing work within a short time.

Apprenticeship programs usually are sponsored by local contractors, trade associations, or by local union-management committees. They provide on-the-job training in addition to the recommended minimum of 144 hours of classroom instruction each year. You may be required to take a written test and pass a physical exam. In the classroom, you will learn applied mathematics, blueprint reading, and safety, and you will probably receive special instruction in layout work and cost estimation.

To be successful in this trade, you should enjoy doing demanding work. You should also take pride in craftsmanship and be able to work without close supervision.

Advancement

With additional training, cement masons, concrete finishers, segmental pavers, or terrazzo workers may become supervisors for masonry contractors or move into construction management, building inspection, or contract estimation. Some become owners of businesses, where they may spend most of their time managing rather than practicing their original trade. Taking business classes will help to prepare workers for opening and operating a business.

Compensation

In 2004, the median hourly earnings of cement masons and concrete finishers were $15.10, with the majority earning between $11.76 and $20.11. The bottom 10 percent earned less than $9.53, and the top 10 percent earned more than $25.89.

The median hourly earnings of terrazzo workers and finishers were $13.45 in 2004. The middle 50 percent earned between $10.44 and $19.57, while the lowest paid earned less than $9.07, and the highest earned more than $25.72.

Wages for cement finishers are either at the same level or above many other skills in construction. Although subject to weather variations, cement finishers usually find enough work inside during severe conditions to prevent a great loss of work time. During good weather, overtime pay very often is the rule. The job of a cement finisher is not easy, but it is generally well compensated and rewarding in terms of the finished product.

Like those of other construction trades workers, earnings of workers in this trade may be reduced on occasion because poor weather and slowdowns in construction activity limit the amount of time they can work. Nonunion workers generally have lower wage rates than union workers. Apprentices usually start at 50 percent to 60 percent of the rate paid to experienced workers. Cement masons often work overtime, with premium pay, because once concrete has been placed, the job must be completed.

Many of these workers belong to unions, mainly the Operative Plasterers' and Cement Masons' International Association of the United States and Canada and the International Union of Bricklayers and Allied Craftworkers. A few terrazzo workers belong to the United Brotherhood of Carpenters and Joiners of the United States.

Job Outlook

Opportunities are expected to be good, particularly for those with the most experience and skills. Employers report difficulty in finding workers with the right skills, as many qualified job seekers often prefer work that is less strenuous and has more comfortable working conditions.

Employment of these workers is expected to grow between 9 percent and 17 percent through 2014, as they will be needed to build new highways, bridges, factories, and other residential and nonresidential structures to meet the demand of a growing population. Additionally, cement masons will be needed to repair and renovate existing highways and bridges, which are deteriorating rapidly, and other aging structures. The increasing use of concrete as a building material, particularly since 9/11, will add to the demand. In addition to job growth, there are expected to be a significant number of retirements over the next decade, which will create more job openings.

As in other construction trades, employment of cement masons, concrete finishers, segmental pavers, and terrazzo workers is sensitive to the fluctuations of the economy. Workers in these trades may experience periods of unemployment when the overall level of construction falls. On the other hand, shortages of these workers may occur in some areas during peak periods of building activity.

Brick Masons, Block Masons, and Stonemasons

Workers in these three categories work in closely related trades creating attractive, durable surfaces and structures. The work varies in complexity, from laying a simple masonry walkway to installing an ornate exterior on a high-rise building.

Brick masons and block masons, who often are called simply *bricklayers*, build and repair walls, floors, partitions, fireplaces, chimneys, and other structures with brick, precast masonry panels, concrete block, and other masonry materials. Some brick masons specialize in installing firebrick linings in industrial furnaces. Stonemasons build stone walls, as well as set stone exteriors and floors. They work with two types of stone: natural cut stone, such as marble, granite, and limestone; and artificial stone made from concrete, marble chips, or other masonry materials. They usually work on nonresidential structures, such as houses of worship, hotels, and office buildings, but they also work on residences.

When building a structure, brick masons use one of two methods, either the corner lead or the corner pole. Using the corner lead method, they begin by constructing a pyramid of bricks at each corner, called a *lead*. After the corner leads are complete, less experienced brick masons fill in the wall between the corners using a line from corner to corner to guide each course, or layer, of brick. Due to the precision needed, corner leads are time-consuming to erect and require the skills of experienced bricklayers.

Because of the expense associated with building corner leads, some brick masons use corner poles, also called *masonry guides*, that enable them to build an entire wall at one time. They fasten the corner poles (posts) in a plumb position to define the wall line and stretch a line between them. This line serves as a guide for each course of brick. They then spread a bed of mortar (a mixture of cement, lime, sand, and water) with a trowel (a flat, bladed metal tool with a handle), place the brick on the mortar bed, and press and tap the brick into place. Depending on blueprint specifications, brick masons either cut bricks with a hammer and chisel or saw them to fit around windows, doors, and other openings. Mortar joints are then finished with jointing tools for a sealed, neat, uniform appearance. Although brick masons typically use steel supports, or lintels, at window and door openings, they sometimes build brick arches, which support and enhance the beauty of the brickwork.

Stonemasons often work from a set of drawings, in which each stone has been numbered for identification. Helpers may locate and carry these prenumbered stones to the masons. A derrick operator using a hoist may be needed to lift large stone pieces into place.

When building a stone wall, masons set the first course of stones into a shallow bed of mortar. They then align the stones with wedges, plumb lines, and levels, and work them into position with a hard rubber mallet. They continue to build the wall by alternating layers of mortar and courses of stone. As the work progresses, they remove the wedges, fill the joints between stones, and use a pointed metal tool, called a *tuck pointer*, to smooth the mortar to an attractive finish. To hold large stones in place, stonemasons attach brackets to the stone and weld or bolt these brackets to anchors in the wall. Finally, they wash the stone with a cleansing solution to remove stains and dry the mortar.

When setting stone floors, often using large and heavy pieces of stone, masons first use a trowel to spread a layer of damp mortar over the surface to be covered. Using crowbars and hard rubber mallets for aligning and leveling, they then set the stone in the mortar bed. To finish, workers fill the joints and clean the stone slabs.

Masons use a special hammer and chisel to cut stone. They cut stone along the grain to make various shapes and sizes, and valuable pieces often are cut with a saw that has a diamond blade. Some masons specialize in setting marble, which, in many respects, is similar to setting large pieces of stone. Brick masons and stonemasons also repair imperfections and cracks, and they replace broken or missing masonry units in walls and floors.

Most nonresidential buildings now are built with walls made of concrete block, brick veneer, stone, granite, marble, tile, or glass. In the past, masons doing nonresidential interior work mainly built block partition walls and elevator shafts, but because many types of masonry and stone are used in the interiors of today's nonresidential structures, these workers now must be more versatile. For example, some brick masons and block masons now install structural insulated wall panels and masonry accessories used in many high-rise buildings.

Refractory masons are brick masons who specialize in installing firebrick and refractory tile in high-temperature boilers, furnaces, cupolas, ladles, and soaking pits in industrial establishments. Most are employed in steel mills, where molten materials flow on refractory beds from furnaces to rolling machines.

Training Required

Like most brick masons, block masons, and stonemasons, you can learn the necessary skills informally, by observing and learning from experienced workers. As an alternative, you can receive training in vocational education schools or from industry-based programs. Another way to learn these skills is through an apprenticeship program, which generally provides the most thorough training. You will need knowledge of algebra, geometry, and mechanical drawing to work in this trade.

If you learn the trade on the job, you will probably start as a helper, laborer, or mason tender and carry materials, move scaffolds, and mix mortar. When the opportunity arises, you can learn from experienced workers how to spread mortar, lay brick and block, or set stone. As you gain experience, you'll make the transition to full-fledged craftworker. Your learning period on the job may last longer than if you are trained in an apprenticeship program. Industry-based training programs offered through construction companies usually last between two and four years.

Most apprenticeships are sponsored by local contractors, trade associations, or local union-management committees. The apprenticeship program requires three years of on-the-job training, in addition to a minimum 144 hours of classroom instruction each year in subjects such as blueprint reading, mathematics, layout work, and sketching. To apply for an apprenticeship, you must be at least seventeen years old and in good physical condition. A high school education is preferable, and courses in mathematics, mechanical drawing, and shop are helpful.

As an apprentice, you will probably start by working with laborers, carrying materials, mixing mortar, and building scaffolds. This period generally lasts about a month and helps you to become familiar with job routines and materials. Next, you'll learn to lay, align, and join brick and block. You may also learn to work with stone and concrete, which enables you to work with more than one masonry material.

Bricklayers who work in nonresidential construction usually work for large contractors, and they receive well-rounded training, normally through an apprenticeship, in all phases of brickwork or stonework. Those who work in residential construction usually work primarily for small contractors and specialize in only one or two aspects of the job.

Advancement

With additional training and experience, brick masons, block masons, and stonemasons may become supervisors for masonry contractors. Some eventually become owners of businesses employing many workers and may spend most of their time as managers rather than as brick masons, block masons, or stonemasons. Others move into closely related areas such as construction management or building inspection.

Compensation

Median hourly earnings of brick masons and block masons in 2004 were $20.07. Most earned between $15.34 and $25.20. The lowest 10 percent earned less than $11.68, and the highest 10 percent earned more than $30.43.

For stonemasons, median hourly earnings in 2004 were $16.82. The majority earned between $12.74 and $21.45. The lowest 10 percent earned less than $9.97, and the highest 10 percent earned more than $27.23.

In Canada, median hourly earnings in 2004 ranged from $18.00 to $28.00. The lowest paid earned between $12.00 and $22.00, and the highest between $26.00 and $31.00.

Earnings for workers in these trades can be reduced on occasion because poor weather and slowdowns in construction activity limit the time they can work. Apprentices or helpers usually start at about

50 percent of the wage rate paid to experienced workers. Pay increases as apprentices gain experience and learn new skills.

Many workers are members of the International Union of Bricklayers and Allied Craftworkers.

Job Outlook

Job opportunities are expected to be very good through 2014. A large number of masons are expected to retire over the next decade, and in some areas there are not enough applicants for the skilled masonry jobs to replace those who are leaving.

Jobs are also expected to increase as population and business growth create a need for new houses, industrial facilities, schools, hospitals, offices, and other structures. Also stimulating demand will be the need to restore a growing stock of old masonry buildings, as well as the increasing use of brick and stone for decorative work on building fronts and in lobbies and foyers. Brick exteriors should remain very popular, reflecting a growing preference for durable exterior materials requiring little maintenance.

Employment of brick masons, block masons, and stonemasons, like that of many other construction workers, is sensitive to changes in the economy. When the level of construction activity falls, workers in these trades can experience periods of unemployment.

Roofers

A leaky roof can damage ceilings, walls, and furnishings. To protect buildings and their contents from water damage, roofers repair and install roofs made of a variety of materials, such as tar or asphalt and gravel; rubber or thermoplastic; metal; or shingles made of asphalt, slate, fiberglass, wood, tile, or other material. The majority of work for this trade comes from repair and reroofing, which is replacing old roofs on existing buildings.

There are two types of roofs, low- and steep-sloped. Roofs considered low-slope rise four inches per horizontal foot or less, and steep-slope roofs increase more than four inches per horizontal foot. Most commercial, industrial, and apartment buildings have low-slope roofs. Most houses have steep-slope roofs. Some roofers work on both types; others specialize.

Most low-slope roofs are covered with several layers of materials. Roofers first put a layer of insulation on the roof deck and then spread a coat of molten bitumen, which is a tarlike substance, over the insulation. Next they install partially overlapping layers of roofing felt, a fabric saturated in bitumen, over the surface. Using a mop, they spread hot bitumen over the surface and under the next layer, which seals the seams and makes the surface watertight. Roofers repeat these steps to build up the desired number of layers, called *plies*. The top layer either is glazed to make a smooth finish or has gravel embedded in the hot bitumen to create a rough surface.

An increasing number of low-slope roofs are covered with a single-ply membrane of waterproof rubber or thermoplastic compounds. Roofers roll these sheets over the roof's insulation and seal the seams. Adhesive, mechanical fasteners, or stone ballast hold the sheets in place. A small but growing number of flat-roofed buildings are now having "green" roofs installed. A green roof begins with a single or multi-ply waterproof system. After it is proven to be leak free, a root barrier is placed onto it, and then layers of soil, in which trees and grass are planted. Roofers are generally responsible for making sure the roof is watertight and can withstand the weight and water needs of the plantings.

Most residential steep-slope roofs are covered with shingles. To apply shingles, roofers first lay, cut, and tack three-foot strips of roofing felt lengthwise over the entire surface. Then, starting from the bottom edge, they staple or nail overlapping rows of shingles to the roof. Workers measure and cut the felt and shingles to fit intersecting roof surfaces and to fit around vent pipes and chimneys. Wherever two roof surfaces intersect, or shingles reach a vent pipe or chimney, roofers cement or nail flashing strips of metal or shingle over the joints to make them watertight. Finally, they cover exposed nail heads with roofing cement or caulking to prevent water leakage. Roofers who use tile, metal shingles, or shakes follow a similar process.

Because of their expertise in waterproofing roofs, some roofers also waterproof and damp-proof masonry and concrete walls and floors, including foundations. To prepare surfaces for waterproofing, they hammer and chisel away rough spots, or remove them with a rubbing brick, before applying a coat of liquid waterproofing compound. They also may paint or spray surfaces with a waterproofing material or attach waterproofing membrane to surfaces. When damp-proofing, they usually spray a bitumen-based coating on interior or exterior surfaces. Roofers also install equipment that requires cutting through roofs, such as ventilation ducts and attic fans.

Training Required

Most roofers acquire their skills informally by working as helpers for experienced roofers and by taking some employer-provided classes. When you start out as a trainee, you will carry equipment and material and erect scaffolds and hoists. Within two or three months, you'll be taught to measure, cut, and fit roofing materials and later, to lay asphalt or fiberglass shingles. Because some roofing materials are used infrequently, it can take several years for you to gain sufficient experience working on all the various types of roofing applications.

You may also choose one of the three-year apprenticeship programs administered by local union-management committees representing roofing contractors and locals of the United Union of Roofers, Waterproofers, and Allied Workers. These programs generally consist of a minimum of two thousand hours of on-the-job training annually, plus a minimum of 144 hours of classroom instruction a year in subjects such as tools and their use, arithmetic, and safety. On-the-job training for apprentices is similar to that for helpers, except that the apprenticeship program is more structured. Apprentices also learn to damp-proof and waterproof walls.

Good physical condition and good balance are essential for roofers, along with no fear of heights. A high school education, or its equivalent, is helpful, as are courses in mechanical drawing and basic mathematics. Most apprentices must be at least eighteen years of age. Experience with metalworking is helpful for workers who install metal roofing.

Advancement

Roofers may advance to supervisor or estimator for a roofing contractor. Some choose to become contractors themselves.

Compensation

Roofers had median hourly earnings of $14.83 in 2004. While the majority earned between $11.54 and $19.80, the lowest paid earned less than $9.41, and the highest earned more than $25.59.

The median hourly earnings of roofers in the foundation, structure, and building exterior contractors industry were $14.90.

Apprentices usually start at about 40 percent to 50 percent of the rate that is paid to experienced roofers, and they receive periodic raises as they acquire the skills of the trade. Earnings for roofers are reduced on occasion because poor weather limits the time they can work.

Some roofers are members of the United Union of Roofers, Waterproofers, and Allied Workers.

Job Outlook

Job opportunities for roofers should be good through the year 2014, primarily because of the need to replace workers who leave the occupation. The proportion of roofers who leave the job each year is higher than in most construction trades; roofing work is hot, strenuous, and dirty, and a significant number of workers treat roofing as a temporary job until something better comes along. Some leave the occupation to go into other construction trades.

Because roofs deteriorate faster and are more susceptible to weather damage than most other parts of buildings and periodically need to be repaired or replaced, this trade has a much higher proportion of repair and replacement work than most other construction occupations. Thus demand for roofers is less susceptible to downturns in the economy than demand for some other trades. In addition to repair and reroofing work on the growing stock of buildings, new construction of industrial, commercial, and residential buildings will add to the demand for roofers. Jobs should be easiest to find during spring and summer, when most roofing is done.

A Final Word

If you like to work outdoors and have the basic skills needed for one of the interesting exterior trades, you may find a career that allows you to be involved in the preparation and structural erection of buildings. However, be sure to carefully evaluate your interests and preferences before committing to one of these trades, because they all involve heavy work and can be quite demanding, but the rewards can be significant.

5

INTERIOR TRADES

THE PAINTERS, PAPERHANGERS, and tile setters who provide some of the finishing decorative touches to building projects work indoors. Read on to learn about the requirements for these trades.

Painters and Paperhangers

Paint and wall coverings make surfaces clean, attractive, and bright. In addition, paints and other sealers protect exterior surfaces from wear caused by exposure to the weather.

Painters apply paint, stain, varnish, and other finishes to buildings and other structures. They choose the right paint or finish for the surface to be covered, taking into account durability, ease of handling, method of application, and customers' wishes. They first prepare the surfaces to be covered so that the paint will adhere properly, which may require removing the old coat of paint by stripping, sanding, wire brushing, burning, or water and abrasive blasting. On new surfaces, they apply a primer or sealer to prepare the surface for the finish coat. They also mix paints and match colors, relying on knowledge of paint composition and color harmony. In large paint shops or hardware stores, these functions are automated.

There are several ways to apply paint and similar coverings, and painters must be able to choose the right paint applicator for each job, depending on the surface to be covered, the characteristics of the finish, and other factors. Some jobs need only a good bristle brush with a soft, tapered edge; others require a dip or fountain pressure roller; still others can best be done using a paint sprayer. Many jobs need several types of applicators. The right tools for each job not only expedite the painter's work but also produce the most attractive surface.

When working on tall buildings, painters erect scaffolding, including *swing stages*, which are scaffolds suspended by ropes or cables attached to roof hooks. When painting steeples and other conical structures, they use a *bosun's chair*, a swinglike device.

Paperhangers cover walls and ceilings with decorative wall coverings made of paper, vinyl, or fabric. They first prepare the surface to be covered by applying *sizing*, which seals the surface and makes the covering adhere better. When redecorating, they may first remove the old covering by soaking, steaming, or applying solvents. When necessary, they patch holes and take care of other imperfections before hanging the new wall covering.

After the surface has been prepared, paperhangers must prepare the paste or other adhesive. Then they measure the area to be covered, check the covering for flaws, cut the covering into strips of the proper size, and closely examine the pattern to match it when the strips are hung. Much of this process can now be handled by specialized equipment.

The next step is to brush or roll the adhesive onto the back of the covering, if needed, and to then place the strips on the wall or ceiling, making sure the pattern is matched, the strips are hung straight, and the edges are butted together to make tight, closed seams. Finally, paperhangers smooth the strips to remove bubbles and wrinkles, trim the top and bottom with a razor knife, and wipe off any excess adhesive.

Training Required

Painting and paperhanging are learned mostly through on-the-job training and by working as a helper to an experienced worker. However, there are a number of formal and informal training programs that will provide you with more thorough instruction and a better career foundation. Besides apprenticeships, you can learn skills by attending technical schools, which take about a year to complete. You can also receive training through local vocational high schools.

If available, apprenticeships are usually the best way to enter the profession. They generally consist of two to four years of on-the-job training, supplemented by 144 hours of related classroom instruction each year. To apply for an apprenticeship, you must be at least eighteen years old and in good physical condition, with a high school education or its equivalent. As an apprentice, you will receive instruction in color harmony, use and care of tools and equipment, surface preparation, application techniques, paint mixing and matching, characteristics of different finishes, blueprint reading, wood finishing, and safety.

Whether a painter learns the trade through a formal apprenticeship or informally as a helper, on-the-job instruction covers similar skill areas. Working as a trainee under the direction of experienced painters, you will carry supplies, erect scaffolds, and do simple painting and surface preparation tasks while you learn about paint and painting equipment. As you gain experience, you'll learn to prepare surfaces for painting and paperhanging, to mix paints, and to apply paint and wall coverings efficiently and neatly. Near the end of the training, you may learn decorating concepts, color coordination, and cost-estimating techniques. In addition to learning craft skills, you must become familiar with safety and health regulations so that your work complies with the law.

Advancement

Painters and paperhangers may advance to supervisory or estimating jobs with painting and decorating contractors. Many establish their own businesses. For those who would like to advance, it is increasingly important to be able to communicate in both English and Spanish in order to relay instructions and safety precautions to workers with limited English skills; Spanish speaking workers make up a large part of the construction workforce in many areas. Painting contractors need good English skills to deal with clients and subcontractors.

Compensation

In 2004, median hourly earnings of painters in construction and maintenance were $14.55, with the majority earning between $11.59 and $19.04. The lowest paid earned less than $9.47; the highest earned more than $25.11.

In 2004, median earnings for paperhangers were $15.73. The middle 50 percent earned between $12.23 and $20.71, while the lowest 10 percent earned less than $9.57, and the highest earned more than $26.58.

Earnings for painters may be reduced on occasion because of bad weather and the short-term nature of many construction jobs. Hourly wage rates for apprentices usually start at 40 to 50 percent of the rate for experienced workers and increase periodically.

Some painters and paperhangers are members of the International Brotherhood of Painters and Allied Trades. Some maintenance painters are members of other unions.

Job Outlook

Job prospects should be excellent because each year thousands of painters retire or leave for jobs in other occupations. Because there are no strict training requirements for entry into these jobs, many people with limited skills work as painters or helpers for a short time and then move on to other types of work. Many fewer openings will arise for paperhangers because the number of these jobs is comparatively small.

New jobs will also be created as a result of increases in the level of new construction and in the stock of buildings and other structures that require maintenance and renovation. The relatively short life of exterior paints as well as changing color trends will stir demand for painters. Painting is labor-intensive and not susceptible to technological changes that might make workers more productive and slow employment growth. Paperhangers should see slower than average employment growth as easy application materials and reduced demand for paperhanging services limit growth.

Those considering these occupations should expect some periods of unemployment, especially until they gain experience. Many construction projects are of short duration, and construction activity is cyclical and seasonal in nature. However, remodeling, restoration, and maintenance projects often provide many jobs for painters and paperhangers, even when new construction activity declines. The most versatile painters and skilled paperhangers generally are best able to keep working steadily during downturns in the economy.

Carpet and Floor Installers and Finishers

Carpet, tile, and other types of floor coverings not only serve an important basic function in buildings, but their decorative qualities also contribute to the visual appeal. Carpet, floor, and tile installers and finishers lay these floor coverings in homes, offices, hospitals, stores, restaurants, and many other types of buildings. Tile also may be installed on walls and ceilings.

Before installing carpet, carpet installers first inspect the surface to be covered to determine its condition and, if necessary, correct any imperfections that could show through the carpet or cause the carpet to wear unevenly. They must measure the area to be carpeted and plan the layout, keeping in mind expected traffic patterns and placement of seams for best appearance and maximum wear.

When installing wall-to-wall carpet without tacks, installers first fasten a tackless strip to the floor, next to the wall, and then install the padded cushion or underlay. Next, they roll out, measure, mark, and cut the carpet, allowing for two to three inches of extra carpet for the final fitting. Using a device called a *knee kicker*, they position the carpet, stretching it to fit evenly on the floor and snugly against each wall and door threshold. They then cut off the excess carpet. Finally, using a power stretcher, they stretch the carpet, hooking it to the tackless strip to hold it in place. The installers then finish the edges using a wall trimmer.

Because most carpet comes in twelve-foot widths, wall-to-wall installations require installers to join carpet sections together for large rooms. They accomplish this by using heat-taped seams, which are held together by a special plastic tape that is activated by heat.

On special upholstery work, such as stairs, carpet may be held in place with staples. Also, in commercial installations, carpet often is glued directly to the floor or to padding that has been glued to the floor.

Carpet installers use hand tools such as hammers, drills, staple guns, carpet knives, and rubber mallets. They also may use carpet-laying tools, such as carpet shears, knee kickers, wall trimmers, loop pile cutters, heat irons, and power stretchers.

Floor installers and floor layers lay floor coverings such as laminate, linoleum, vinyl, cork, and rubber for decorative purposes or to deaden sounds, absorb shocks, or create air-tight environments. Although they also may install carpet, wood, or tile, that is not their main job. Before installing the floor, they inspect the surface to be covered and, if necessary, correct any imperfections in order to start with a smooth, clean foundation. They measure and cut floor covering materials according to plans or blueprints. Next, they may nail or staple a wood underlayment to the surface or may use an adhesive to cement the foundation material to the floor; the foundation helps to deaden sound and prevents the top floor covering from wearing at board joints. Finally, floor layers install the floor covering to form a tight fit.

After a carpenter installs a new hardwood floor or when a customer wants to refinish an old wood floor, floor sanders and finishers are called in to smooth any imperfections in the wood and apply finish coats of varnish or polyurethane. To remove imperfections and smooth the surface, they will scrape and sand wooden floors using floor-sanding machines. They then inspect the floor and remove excess glue from joints using a knife or wood chisel and may further sand the wood surfaces by hand, using sandpaper. Finally, they apply coats of finish.

Training Required

The vast majority of carpet and floor installers and finishers learn their trade informally on the job. A few attend formal apprenticeship programs that take nearly three years to complete and include on-the-job training as well as related classroom instruction.

Informal training for carpet installers often is sponsored by individual contractors. You will start as a helper and begin with simple assignments, such as installing stripping and padding or helping to stretch newly installed carpet. With experience, you'll take on more difficult assignments, such as measuring, cutting, and fitting.

To learn how to actually lay flooring, you'll begin by learning how to use the tools of the trade. Next you will learn to prepare surfaces to receive flooring, and as you progress, you'll learn to cut and install the various floor coverings.

Some of the attributes you will need to become a carpet or floor installer or finisher are manual dexterity, eye-hand coordination, physical fitness, and a good sense of balance and color. You must also be able to solve arithmetic problems quickly and accurately.

Advancement

Carpet and floor installers and finishers may advance to positions as supervisors or become salespersons or estimators. In these positions, they should be able to identify and estimate the quantity of materials needed to complete a job and accurately estimate how long a job will take to complete and at what cost.

Some carpet installers will become managers for large installation firms. Many workers in this trade who begin working for someone else eventually go into business for themselves as independent subcontractors.

Compensation

In 2004, the median hourly earnings of carpet installers were $16.39. While most earned between $11.94 and $22.20, the lowest paid earned less than $9.16, and the highest earned more than $29.27. Median hourly earnings of carpet installers were $16.55 working for building finishing contractors and $15.43 for home furnishings stores.

Carpet installers are paid either on an hourly basis or by the number of yards of carpet installed. The rates vary widely depending on the geographic location and whether the installer is affiliated with a union.

Median hourly earnings of floor layers except carpet, wood, and hard tiles were $15.68 in 2004. The majority earned between $11.80 and $20.93. The lowest 10 percent earned less than $8.98, and the top 10 percent earned more than $28.09.

Median hourly earnings of floor sanders and finishers were $12.88. Most earned between $10.30 and $16.47, while the lowest 10 percent earned less than $8.91, and the top 10 percent earned more than $21.03.

Apprentices and other trainees usually start out earning about half of what an experienced worker earns, although their wage rate increases as they advance through the training program.

Some carpet and floor installers and finishers belong to the United Brotherhood of Carpenters and Joiners of America and the International Brotherhood of Painters and Allied Trades.

Job Outlook

Employment in this trade is expected to grow between 9 and 17 percent through the year 2014, reflecting the continued need to renovate and refurbish existing structures. However, job growth and opportunities will differ among the individual occupations. Carpet installers, the largest specialty, should have the most job openings due to high turnover. Employment of floor sanders and finishers, a small specialty, is projected to grow only as much as 8 percent due to the increasing use of prefinished hardwood and laminate flooring.

Carpet is expected to increasingly be used as a floor covering in nonresidential structures such as schools, offices, and hospitals. Residences will also continue to use carpet in many areas of the house, although other flooring types are currently more popular. Carpet is also required or highly recommended in many multifamily structures as it provides sound dampening.

Demand for floor sanders and finishers will be primarily based on growth in the residential construction and remodeling market, as home owners increasingly choose hardwood as their flooring of choice. The need to periodically refinish older wood floors will also continue to generate demand, but growth will be slowed by the use of more prefinished hardwood and more durable finishes and laminate products that look like wood. Slow employment growth, together with the small size of this occupation, will result in relatively few job openings for these workers.

Employment in this trade is less sensitive to changes in construction activity than most other trades because much of the work involves replacing worn carpet and other flooring in existing buildings. As a result, these workers tend to be less affected by slowdowns in new construction activity.

Tile Installers and Marble Setters

Tile installers, tile setters, and marble setters are the workers who install the practical and attractive floors, walls, ceilings, countertops, and roof decks that we see in homes and businesses. Tile and marble are durable, impervious to water, and easy to clean, making them a popular building material in hospitals, tunnels, building lobbies, bathrooms, and kitchens.

Prior to installation, tile setters use measuring devices and levels to ensure that the surface is even and that the tile will be placed in a consistent manner. Tile varies in color and shape and ranges in size from one inch to twenty-four or more inches on a side, so tile setters sometimes prearrange tiles on a dry floor according to the intended design. This allows them to examine the pattern, check that they have enough of each type of tile, and determine where they will have to cut tiles to fit the design in the available space. To cover all exposed areas, including corners and around pipes, tubs, and wash basins, they cut tiles to fit with a machine saw or a special cutting tool. To set tile on a flat, solid surface such as drywall, concrete, plaster, or wood, tile setters first use a tooth-edged trowel to spread a *thin set*, or thin layer, of cement adhesive or *mastic*, a very sticky paste. They then properly position the tile and gently tap the surface with their trowel handle, rubber mallet, and/or a small block of wood to seat the tile evenly and firmly.

To apply tile to an area that lacks a solid surface, tile setters nail a support of metal mesh or tile backer board to the wall or ceiling to be tiled. They use a trowel to apply a cement mortar, called a *scratch coat*, onto the metal screen and scratch the surface of the soft mortar with a small tool similar to a rake. After the scratch coat has dried, they apply a brown coat of mortar to level the surface and then apply mortar to the brown coat and place tile onto the surface.

When the cement or mastic has set, tile setters fill the joints with a material called *grout*, which is very fine cement that includes sand for joints one-eighth of an inch and larger. They then apply the grout to the surface with a rubber-edged device called a *grout float* or a *grouting trowel* to dress the joints and remove excess grout. Before the grout sets, they finish the joints with a damp sponge for a uniform appearance.

Marble setters cut and set marble slabs in floors and walls of buildings. They trim and cut marble to specified sizes using a power wet saw, other cutting equipment, or hand tools. After setting the marble in place, they polish the marble to high luster using power tools or by hand.

Training Required

The majority of tile installers and finishers learn their trade informally on the job. A few, mostly tile setters, learn through formal apprenticeship programs that take nearly three years to complete, which include on-the-job training as well as related classroom instruction.

As an on-the-job trainee, you'll start by helping to carry materials and learning about the tools of the trade; you will then learn to prepare the subsurface for tile or marble. As you progress you'll learn to cut the tile and marble to fit the job and to apply grout and sealants used in finishing the materials to give it its final appearance.

To learn the trade, you will need manual dexterity, eye-hand coordination, physical fitness, and a good sense of balance and color. The ability to solve arithmetic problems quickly and accurately also is required.

Advancement

Tile installers and finishers may advance to positions as supervisors or become salespersons or estimators. In these positions, they should be able to identify and estimate the quantity of materials needed to complete a job and accurately estimate how long a job will take to complete and at what cost. Like floor installers, many tile installers and finishers who begin working for someone else eventually go into business for themselves as independent subcontractors.

Compensation

Median hourly earnings of tile and marble setters were $17.02 in 2004, with most earning between $12.69 and $22.59. The lowest 10 percent earned less than $9.85, and the top 10 percent earned more than $29.35. Earnings of tile and marble setters also vary greatly by geographic location and by union membership status.

Apprentices and other trainees usually start out earning about half of what an experienced worker earns, although their wage rate increases as they advance through the training program.

Tile installers and finishers may belong to the United Brotherhood of Carpenters and Joiners of America, and tile setters may join the International Union of Bricklayers and Allied Craftworkers.

Job Outlook

Job prospects in this trade are expected to be good over the next several years, reflecting the continued need to renovate and refurbish existing structures. Tile and marble setters should have faster than average job growth and excellent opportunities as demand for these workers outstrips the supply; however, because it is a small occupation, job openings will be limited.

Demand for tile and marble setters will stem from population and business growth, which will result in more construction of shopping malls, hospitals, schools, restaurants, and other structures in which tile is used extensively. Tile is also becoming more popular as a building material in residential structures, particularly in the growing number of more expensive homes.

Employment is less sensitive to changes in construction activity than most other construction occupations because much of the work involves replacing worn materials in existing buildings. As a result, these workers are less affected by slowdowns in new construction.

Glaziers

Glass serves many uses in our lives. Insulated and specially treated glass keeps in warmed or cooled air and provides good condensation and sound control qualities, while tempered and laminated glass makes doors and windows more secure. In large commercial buildings, glass panels give office buildings a distinctive look while reducing the need for artificial lighting. The creative use of large windows, glass doors, skylights, and sunroom additions makes homes bright, airy, and inviting.

Glaziers are the professionals who are responsible for selecting, cutting, installing, replacing, and removing all types of glass. They generally work on one of several types of projects. Residential glazing involves replacing glass in home windows; installing glass mirrors, shower doors, and bathtub enclosures; and fitting glass for tabletops and display cases. Commercial interior work involves installing items such as heavy, often etched, decorative room dividers or security windows. Glazing projects also may involve replacement of storefront windows for establishments such as supermarkets, auto dealerships, or banks. In the construction of large commercial buildings, glaziers build metal framework extrusions and install glass panels or curtain walls.

Besides working with glass, glaziers also may work with plastics, granite, marble, and other similar materials used as glass substitutes, as well as films or laminates that improve the durability or safety of the glass. They mount steel and aluminum sashes or frames and attach locks and hinges to glass doors.

For most jobs, the glass is precut and mounted in frames at a factory or a contractor's shop, and it arrives at the job site ready for glaziers to position and secure it in place. They may use a crane or hoist with suction cups to lift large, heavy pieces of glass. They then gently guide the glass into position by hand.

Once glaziers have the glass in place, they secure it with mastic, putty, or other pastelike cement or with bolts, rubber gaskets, glazing compound, metal clips, or metal or wood moldings. For some jobs, the glass must be cut manually at the job site. To prepare the glass for cutting, glaziers rest it either on edge on a rack, or "A-frame," or flat against a cutting table, so that they can measure and mark the glass for the cut.

Glaziers cut glass with a special tool that has a small, very hard metal wheel. Using a straightedge as a guide, they press the cutter's wheel firmly on the glass, guiding and rolling it carefully to make a score just below the surface. To help the cutting tool move smoothly across the glass, workers brush a thin layer of oil along the line of the intended cut or dip the cutting tool in oil. Immediately after cutting, the glazier presses on the shorter end of the glass to break it cleanly along the cut.

In addition to hand tools such as glass cutters, suction cups, and glazing knives, glaziers use power tools such as saws, drills, cutters, and grinders. An increasing number of glaziers use computers in the shop or at the job site to improve their layout work and reduce the amount of glass that is wasted.

Training Required

Becoming a skilled glazier usually takes three years of both classroom and on-the-job training. You have a number of different options for obtaining the necessary training. One is to find a job with a contractor who will provide on-the-job training. In this situation you'll start as a helper assisting more experienced workers, and your employer may send you to a trade or vocational school or community college to receive further classroom training.

Some employers offer formal apprenticeships that combine on-the-job training with related classroom instruction. You must be at least eighteen years old and meet local requirements to apply for an apprenticeship. Most programs last three years, but the length may vary depending on your skill level.

On the job as an apprentice or helper, you'll start by carrying glass and cleaning up debris in glass shops, and you may practice cutting on discarded glass. After a while, you will be given an opportunity to cut glass for a job and assist experienced workers on simple installation jobs. By working with experienced glaziers, you'll eventually acquire the skills of a fully qualified glazier. On the job you'll also learn to use the tools and equipment of the trade; handle, measure, cut, and install glass and metal framing; cut and fit moldings; and install and balance glass doors. In the classroom, you will learn about glass and installation techniques as well as basic mathematics, blueprint reading and sketching, general construction techniques, safety practices and first aid.

Because most glaziers do not learn the trade through a formal apprenticeship program, some associations offer a series of written examinations that certify a worker's competency to perform glazier work at three progressively more difficult levels of proficiency. These levels include Level I Glazier; Level II Commercial Interior/Residential Glazier or Storefront/Curtainwall Glazier; and Level III Master Glazier. There also is a certification program for auto-glass repair.

To become a glazier, you'll need manual dexterity, eye-hand coordination, physical fitness, and a good sense of balance. The ability to solve arithmetic problems quickly and accurately also is required.

Advancement

Advancement generally consists of increases in pay for most glaziers, although some advance to supervisory jobs or become contractors or estimators. Glaziers may advance to glazier supervisor or general construction supervisor positions. Others may become independent contractors. Supervisors and contractors need good communication skills to deal with clients and subcontractors; they should be able to identify and estimate the quantity of materials needed to do the job and accurately estimate how long the job will take to complete and at what cost. For those who would like to advance, it is increasingly important to be able to communicate in both English and Spanish in order to relay instructions and safety precautions to workers with limited understanding of English.

Compensation

In 2004, median hourly earnings of glaziers were $15.70. Most earned between $12.08 and $21.58, while the lowest paid earned less than $9.73, and the highest earned more than $30.36. Median hourly earnings in the foundation, structure, and building exterior contractors industry, where most glass shops are found, were $16.10.

Glaziers covered by union contracts generally earn more than their nonunion peers. Apprentice wage rates usually start at 40 percent to 50 percent of the rate paid to experienced glaziers and increase as they gain experience in the field. Because glaziers can lose time due to weather conditions and fluctuations in construction activity, their overall earnings may be lower than their hourly wages suggest.

Some glaziers employed in construction are members of the International Union of Painters and Allied Trades.

Job Outlook

Job opportunities for glaziers are expected to be good as some employers report difficulty in finding qualified workers. In addition, employment is expected to grow between 9 and 17 percent through the year 2014.

Employment of glaziers is expected to increase as a result of growth in residential and nonresidential construction. Demand also will be spurred by the continuing need to modernize and repair existing structures, which often involves installing new windows. Home owners also are preferring rooms with more sunlight and are adding sunrooms and skylights to houses. Demand for specialized safety glass and glass coated with protective laminates is also growing in response to a higher need for security and the need to withstand hurricanes, particularly in many commercial and government buildings.

Like other construction trades workers, glaziers should expect to experience periods of unemployment resulting from the limited duration of construction projects and the cyclical nature of the industry. During bad economic times, job openings for glaziers are reduced as the level of construction declines. However, construction activity varies from area to area, so job openings fluctuate with local economic conditions. Employment opportunities should be greatest in metropolitan areas, where most glazing contractors and glass shops are located.

A Final Word

If your preference runs to working indoors, and you have the desire to be involved in the finished product, you might find success as a painter, paperhanger, tile setter, or glazier. You'll need patience and attention to detail for these jobs, so be sure to think carefully about whether these trades are for you.

6

LICENSED AND RELATED TRADES

THERE ARE SOME trades that require more than on-the-job training or even a formal apprenticeship. Members of certain construction building trades must be licensed to work in their field. Licensing is usually required of those trades that have the most potential for damage or injury if done improperly, such as electricians, plumbers, and elevator installers. To understand the need for licensing, you need only think for a moment about what might happen if a building is improperly wired, the plumbing is installed incorrectly, and the elevators have not been properly set.

In this chapter we will discuss the three primary trades that require workers to be licensed.

Electricians

Where would we be without electricity? The very thought of a power failure causes most of us to panic, because we depend on electricity to keep so many components of our homes and businesses running. Whether it's climate control, security, or communications, we rely heavily on systems that are run electrically.

Electricians are the professionals who bring the electricity into our homes and offices. Most specialize in construction or maintenance work, although a growing number do both. Those who specialize in construction work primarily install wiring systems into new homes, businesses, and factories, but they also rewire or upgrade existing electrical systems as needed. Those specializing in maintenance work primarily maintain and upgrade existing electrical systems and repair electrical equipment.

When installing new systems, electricians work with blueprints that indicate the locations of circuits, outlets, load centers, panel boards, and other equipment. They must follow the National Electrical Code and comply with state and local building codes when they install these systems. Electricians working in Canada must follow the Canadian Electrical Code as well as provincial and local codes. Regulations vary depending on the setting and require various types of installation procedures.

In a typical house, an electrician's work starts at the service line, which usually comes from the rear lot line; it may be either overhead or underground and is run up to the side of the house. The electrician places the distribution panel in the utility area of the house, where a circuit breaker–type panel is installed. For instance, a 50-ampere, 230-volt circuit serves the range and oven; a 20-ampere, 115-volt circuit serves the dishwasher and garbage disposal; a 30-ampere, 230-volt circuit for the dryer; a 20-ampere, 230-volt circuit for a hot water heater; a 15-ampere, 115-volt circuit for the furnace. ,

The electrician then cuts holes through studs, plates, or joists to run wires throughout the house. Once the rough wiring is in place, a local electrical inspector must inspect and approve the job.

After the wiring is completed, the drywall is hung, and the kitchen cabinets have been installed, the electrician has to hook up all of the equipment. Switches, receptacles, and electrical fixtures are also installed at this time. The job is finished when the electrician receives final approval from an electrical inspector.

When electricians install wiring systems in factories and commercial settings, they first place conduit (pipe or tubing) inside partitions, walls, or other concealed areas that are designated by the blueprints. They also fasten small metal or plastic boxes to the walls that will house electrical switches and outlets, and they pull insulated wires or cables through the conduit to complete circuits between these boxes. The gauge and number of wires installed in all settings depends on the load and end use of that part of the electrical system. The greater the diameter of the wire, the higher the voltage and amperage that can flow through it.

Electricians connect all types of wire to circuit breakers, transformers, outlets, or other components and join the wires in boxes with various specially designed connectors. During installation, they use hand tools such as conduit benders, screwdrivers, pliers, knives, hacksaws, and wire strippers, as well as power tools such as drills and saws. After they finish installing the wiring, they use testing equipment, including ammeters, ohmmeters, voltmeters, and oscilloscopes, to check the circuits for proper connections, ensuring electrical compatibility and safety of components.

Maintenance work varies depending on where the electrician is employed. Those who specialize in residential work do a wide variety of electrical work for home owners, performing work that includes rewiring a home and replacing an old fuse box with a new circuit breaker box to accommodate any additional appliances or installing new lighting and other electric household items, such as ceiling fans. Those who work in large factories may repair motors, transformers, generators, and electronic controllers on machine tools and industrial robots. In office buildings and small plants, they repair all types of electrical equipment.

Maintenance electricians working in factories, hospitals, and other settings install new electrical equipment and repair older equipment when necessary, replacing items such as circuit breakers, fuses, switches, electrical and electronic components, or wire. Electricians also periodically inspect equipment to check for proper operation and to troubleshoot for any potential problems. They also advise management whether continued operation of equipment could be hazardous, and they may work alongside engineers, engineering technicians, line installers and repairers, or industrial machinery installation, repair, and maintenance workers.

Although primarily classified as work for line installers and repairers, electricians also may install low-voltage wiring systems in addition to wiring a building's electrical system. Low-voltage wiring involves voice, data, and video wiring systems, such as those for telephones, computers and related equipment, intercoms, and fire alarm and security systems. Electricians also may install coaxial or fiber optic cable for computers and other telecommunications equipment and electronic controls for industrial uses.

Training Required

Most electricians learn their trade through apprenticeship programs that combine on-the-job training with related classroom instruction. These programs are sponsored by joint training committees made up of local unions of the International Brotherhood of Electrical Workers and local chapters of the National Electrical Contractors Association; the company management committees of individual electrical contracting companies; or local chapters of the Associated Builders and Contractors and the Independent Electrical Contractors Association. The comprehensive training offered by these programs will qualify you to do both maintenance and construction work.

To apply for an apprenticeship, you must be at least eighteen years old and have a high school diploma or its equivalent. You should have good math and English skills, because most instruction manuals are in English. You may also have to pass a test and meet other requirements. Apprenticeship programs usually last four years and each year include at least 144 hours of classroom instruction and two thousand hours of on-the-job training. In the classroom, you'll learn electrical theory and installing and maintaining electrical systems. You will also take classes in blueprint reading, mathematics, electrical code requirements, and safety and first aid practices, and you will receive specialized training in soldering, communications, fire alarm systems, and cranes and elevators. On the job, you'll work under the supervision of experienced electricians, where you will start by drilling holes, setting anchors, and attaching conduit. Later, you'll measure, fabricate, and install conduit, as well as install, connect, and test wiring, outlets, and switches. You will learn to set up and draw diagrams for entire electrical systems. To complete the apprenticeship and become an electrician, you must demonstrate mastery of the electrician's work.

You also have the option to complete your classroom training before looking for a job. Training to become an electrician is offered by a number of public and private vocational-technical schools and training academies in affiliation with local unions and contractor organizations. Employers often hire students who complete these programs and usually start them at a more advanced level than those without the training. You may begin your career by first working as a helper, assisting electricians setting up job sites, gathering materials, and doing other nonelectrical work, before entering an apprenticeship program.

To become an electrician, you should have manual dexterity, eye-hand coordination, physical fitness, and a good sense of balance. The ability to solve arithmetic problems quickly and accurately also is required, and you'll need good color vision because electrical wires must be identified by color.

You will need to be licensed to work as an electrician in most localities. Although licensing requirements vary, you'll probably have to pass an exam that tests your knowledge of electrical theory, the National Electrical Code, and local electric and building codes. To work in Canada, you must exhibit competence in the Canadian Electrical Code/Building Code and Industrial Electrical Safety.

Once you gain experience, you will most likely take periodic courses offered by your employer or union to keep abreast of changes in the national codes and new materials or methods of installation. For example, classes on installing low-voltage voice, data, and video systems have recently become common as these systems have become more prevalent.

Advancement

Experienced electricians can advance to jobs as supervisors. In construction they also may become project managers or construction superintendents. Those with sufficient capital and management skills may start their own contracting business, although this may require an electrical contractor's license. Many electricians also become electrical inspectors. Supervisors and contractors should be able to identify and estimate the correct type and quantity of materials needed to complete a job and accurately estimate how long a job will take to complete and at what cost.

The ability to communicate in both English and Spanish is increasingly important for advancement, in order to relay instructions and information to the large number of Spanish-speaking workers who make up much of the workforce. Spanish-speaking workers who want to advance in this occupation need very good English skills to understand instruction presented in classes and installation instructions, which are usually written in English and are highly technical.

Compensation

In 2004, median hourly earnings of electricians were $20.33. The majority earned between $15.43 and $26.90, while the lowest paid earned less than $12.18, and the highest earned more than $33.63.

The average earnings of electricians in Canada in 2004 ranged from $20.00 to $22.00. The lowest earnings were between $10.00 and $13.00; the highest ranged from $27.00 to $31.00.

Apprentices usually start at between 40 percent and 50 percent of the rate paid to fully trained electricians, depending on experience. As apprentices become more skilled, they receive periodic pay increases throughout the course of their training.

Some electricians are members of the International Brotherhood of Electrical Workers. Among unions representing maintenance electricians are the International Brotherhood of Electrical Workers; the International Union of Electronic, Electrical, Salaried, Machine, and Furniture Workers; the International Association of Machinists and Aerospace Workers; the International Union, United Automobile, Aircraft, and Agricultural Implement Workers of America; and the United Steelworkers of America.

Job Outlook

The outlook for electricians is expected to be good over the next several years. As the population and economy grow, more electricians will be needed to install and maintain electrical devices and wiring in homes, factories, offices, and other structures. New technologies also are expected to continue to stimulate the demand for this trade. For example, buildings need to increasingly accommodate the use of computers and telecommunications equipment. Also, the increasing prevalence in factories of robots and other automated manufacturing systems will require the installation and maintenance of more complex wiring systems. Additional jobs will be created as older structures are rehabilitated and retrofitted, which usually require that they be updated to meet current electrical codes.

Employment of construction electricians, like that of many other construction workers, is sensitive to changes in the economy. This results from the limited duration of construction projects and the cyclical nature of the construction industry. During economic downturns, job openings for electricians are reduced as the level of construction activity declines. Apprenticeship opportunities also are less plentiful during these periods.

Although employment of maintenance electricians is steadier than that of construction electricians, those working in the automotive and other manufacturing industries that are sensitive to cyclical swings in the economy may be laid off during recessions. Also, opportunities for maintenance electricians may be limited in many industries by the increased contracting out for electrical services to reduce operating costs and increase productivity. However, increased job opportunities for electricians in electrical contracting firms should partially offset job losses in other industries.

Plumbers, Pipe Layers, Pipe Fitters, and Steamfitters

Most of us are familiar with plumbers, who come to our homes to unclog a drain or install an appliance. In addition to these activities, however, pipe layers, plumbers, pipe fitters, and steamfitters install, maintain, and repair many different types of pipe systems. For example, some systems move water to a municipal water treatment plant and then to residential, commercial, and public buildings. Others dispose of waste, provide gas to stoves and furnaces, or provide for heating and cooling needs. Pipe systems in power plants carry the steam that powers huge turbines. Pipes also are used in manufacturing plants to move material through the production process. Specialized piping systems are very important in both pharmaceutical and computer-chip manufacturing.

Although pipe-laying, plumbing, pipe-fitting, and steamfitting sometimes are considered a single trade, workers generally specialize in one of four areas:

• Pipe layers lay clay, concrete, plastic, or cast-iron pipe for drains, sewers, water mains, and oil or gas lines. First, they prepare and grade the trenches either manually or with machines. After laying the pipe, they weld, glue, cement, or otherwise join the pieces together.

• Plumbers install and repair the water, waste disposal, drainage, and gas systems in homes and commercial and industrial buildings. They also install plumbing fixtures, such as bathtubs, showers, sinks, and toilets, and appliances, such as dishwashers and water heaters.

• Pipe fitters install and repair both high- and low-pressure pipe systems used in manufacturing, in generating electricity, and in heating and cooling buildings. They also install automatic controls that are increasingly being used to regulate these systems. Some specialize in only one type of system.

• Steamfitters install pipe systems that move liquids or gases under high pressure. Sprinkler fitters install automatic fire sprinkler systems in buildings.

Workers in this trade use many different materials and construction techniques, depending on the type of project. For example, residential water systems incorporate copper, steel, and plastic pipe that can be handled and installed by one or two plumbers. Municipal sewerage systems, on the other hand, are made of large cast-iron pipes; installation normally requires crews of pipe fitters. Despite these differences, all workers in the trade must be able to follow building plans or blueprints and instructions from supervisors, lay out the job, and work efficiently with the materials and tools of their trade.

When construction plumbers install piping in a new house, for example, they work from blueprints or drawings that show the planned locations of pipes, plumbing fixtures, and appliances. Recently, plumbers have become more involved in the design process, because their knowledge of codes and the operation of plumbing systems can cut costs. They first lay out the job to fit the piping into the structure of the house with the least waste of material, and then they measure and mark areas in which pipes will be installed and connected. Construction plumbers also check for obstructions such as electrical wiring and, if necessary, plan the pipe installation around the problem.

Sometimes, plumbers have to cut holes in the walls, ceilings, and floors of a house. For some systems, they may hang steel supports from ceiling joists to hold the pipe in place. To assemble a system, plumbers use saws, pipe cutters, and pipe-bending machines to cut and bend lengths of pipe that they connect with fittings, using methods that depend on the type of pipe used. For plastic pipe, they connect the sections and fittings with adhesives; for copper pipe, they slide a fitting over the end of the pipe and solder it in place.

After the piping is in place in the house, plumbers install the fixtures and appliances and connect the system to the outside water or sewer lines. Finally, using pressure gauges, they check the system to ensure that the plumbing works properly.

Training Required

There are a number of ways to enter this profession. Most residential and industrial plumbers get their training in career and technical schools and community colleges and from on-the-job training. Those who work mainly for commercial enterprises are usually trained through formal apprenticeship programs.

Apprenticeship programs generally provide the most comprehensive training available for these jobs. They are administered by union locals and their affiliated companies or by nonunion contractor organizations, including the United Association of Journeymen and Apprentices of the Plumbing and Pipefitting Industry of the United States and Canada; local employers of the Mechanical Contractors Association of America, the National Association of Plumbing-Heating-Cooling Contractors, or the National Fire Sprinkler Association; the Associated Builders and Contractors; the National Association of Plumbing-Heating-Cooling Contractors; the American Fire Sprinkler Association; or the Home Builders Institute of the National Association of Home Builders.

Both union and nonunion apprenticeships consist of four or five years of on-the-job training, in addition to at least 144 hours per year of related classroom instruction. Your classroom studies will include drafting and blueprint reading, mathematics, applied physics and chemistry, safety, and local plumbing codes and regulations. On the job, you'll first learn basic skills, such as identifying grades and types of pipe, using the tools of the trade, and safely unloading materials. As you gain experience, you'll learn how to work with various types of pipe and how to install different piping systems and plumbing fixtures. Apprenticeship will give you a thorough knowledge of all aspects of the trade.

You must be at least eighteen years old and in good physical condition to apply for union and nonunion apprenticeships, and you may need a high school diploma or equivalent. Armed forces training in the trade is considered very good preparation, and you may even be given credit for such previous experience when entering a civilian apprenticeship program. Secondary or postsecondary courses in shop, plumbing, general mathematics, drafting, blueprint reading, computers, and physics also are good preparation.

Although there are no uniform national licensing requirements in the United States or Canada, most communities require plumbers to be licensed. Licensing requirements vary from area to area, but most localities require workers to pass an examination that tests their knowledge of the trade and of local plumbing codes. Check with your state or province for requirements in your area.

Advancement

With additional training, workers in this trade may become supervisors for mechanical and plumbing contractors. Others, especially plumbers, go into business for themselves, often starting as a self-employed plumber working from home. Some eventually open their own businesses that employ many workers and may spend most of their time as managers rather than as plumbers. Others move into closely related areas such as construction management or building inspection.

Compensation

In 2004, median hourly earnings of pipe layers were $13.68. The majority earned between $11.05 and $18.69, while the lowest paid earned less than $9.19, and the highest earned more than $25.07.

Also in 2004, median hourly earnings of plumbers, pipe fitters, and steamfitters were $19.85. Most earned between $15.01 and $26.67. The lowest 10 percent earned less than $11.62, and the highest 10 percent earned more than $33.72.

Workers in this trade in Canada had average hourly earnings in 2004 of $21.00. The lowest earners had average wages of $10.00 to $13.00; the highest ranged from $29.00 to $31.00.

Apprentices usually begin at about 50 percent of the wage rate paid to experienced workers, and wages increase periodically as skills improve. After an initial waiting period, apprentices receive the same benefits as experienced pipe layers, plumbers, pipe fitters, and steamfitters.

Many pipe layers, plumbers, pipe fitters, and steamfitters are members of the United Association of Journeymen and Apprentices of the Plumbing and Pipefitting Industry of the United States and Canada.

Job Outlook

Job opportunities are expected to be excellent, as demand for skilled pipe layers, plumbers, pipe fitters, and steamfitters is expected to outpace the supply of workers trained in this craft. Many employers report difficulty finding potential workers with the right qualifications. In addition, many people currently working in these trades are expected to retire over the next ten years, which will create additional job openings.

Demand for plumbers will stem from new construction and building renovation. Bath remodeling, in particular, is expected to continue to grow and create more jobs, and repair and maintenance of existing residential systems will keep plumbers employed. Demand for pipe fitters and steamfitters will be driven by maintenance activities for places with extensive systems of pipes, such as power plants, water and wastewater treatment plants, office buildings, and factories. Opportunities for pipe layers will stem from the building of new water and sewer lines and pipelines to new oil and gas fields. Demand for sprinkler fitters will increase due to changes to state and local rules for fire protection in homes and businesses.

Traditionally, many organizations with extensive pipe systems have employed their own plumbers or pipe fitters to maintain equipment and keep systems running smoothly. But, to reduce labor costs, many no longer employ full-time, in-house plumbers or pipe fitters. Instead, when they need a plumber, they rely on workers provided under service contracts by plumbing and pipe-fitting contractors.

Construction projects generally provide only temporary employment. When a project ends, some workers in this trade may be unemployed until they can begin work on a new project, although most companies are trying to limit these periods of unemployment to retain workers. In addition, the jobs of pipe layers, plumbers, pipe fitters, and steamfitters are generally less sensitive to changes in economic conditions than jobs in other construction trades. Even when construction activity declines, maintenance, rehabilitation, and replacement of existing piping systems, as well as the increasing installation of fire sprinkler systems, provide many jobs for pipe layers, plumbers, pipe fitters, and steamfitters.

Elevator Installers and Repairers

Elevator installers and repairers, also called *elevator constructors* or *mechanics*, assemble, install, and replace elevators, escalators, dumbwaiters, moving walkways, and similar equipment in new and old buildings. Once the equipment is in service, they maintain and repair it as well. They also are responsible for modernizing older equipment.

To install, repair, and maintain modern elevators, which are almost all electronically controlled, these mechanics must have a thorough knowledge of electronics, electricity, and hydraulics. Many elevators are controlled with microprocessors, which are programmed to analyze traffic conditions so as to dispatch cars in the most efficient manner. With these computer controls, it is possible to get the greatest amount of service with the fewest number of cars.

To install a new elevator, mechanics begin by studying blueprints to determine the equipment needed to install rails, machinery, car enclosures, motors, pumps, cylinders, and plunger foundations. Once this has been done, they work on scaffolding or platforms to install, bolt, or weld steel rails to the walls of the shaft to guide the elevator.

Elevator installers put in electrical wires and controls by running tubing, called *conduit*, along a shaft's walls from floor to floor. Once the conduit is in place, mechanics pull plastic-covered electrical wires through it. They then install electrical components and related devices required at each floor and at the main control panel in the machine room.

Installers bolt or weld together the steel frame of an elevator car at the bottom of the shaft; install the car's platform, walls, and doors; and attach guide shoes and rollers to minimize the lateral motion of the car as it travels through the shaft. They also install the outer doors and door frames at the elevator entrances on each floor.

For cabled elevators, these workers install geared or gearless machines with a traction drive wheel that guides and moves heavy steel cables connected to the elevator car and counterweight. (The counterweight moves in the opposite direction from the car and balances most of the weight of the car to reduce the weight that the elevator's motor must lift.) Elevator installers also install elevators in which a car sits on a hydraulic plunger that is driven by a pump. The plunger pushes the elevator car up from underneath, similar to a lift in an auto service station.

Escalators are installed by placing the steel framework and electrically powered stairs and tracks and installing associated motors and electrical wiring. In addition to elevators and escalators, installers and repairers also may install devices such as dumbwaiters and material lifts, which are similar to elevators in design, as well as moving walkways, stair lifts, and wheelchair lifts.

The most highly skilled elevator installers and repairers, called *adjusters*, specialize in fine-tuning all the equipment after installation. They make sure that an elevator is working according to specifications and is stopping correctly at each floor within a specified time. Once an elevator is operating properly, it must be maintained and serviced regularly to keep it in safe working condition. Elevator installers and repairers generally do preventive maintenance, such as oiling and greasing moving parts, replacing worn parts, testing equipment with meters and gauges, and adjusting equipment for optimal performance. They also troubleshoot and may be called to do emergency repairs.

A service crew usually handles major repairs, which include replacing cables, elevator doors, or machine bearings. This may require the use of cutting torches or rigging equipment, tools that an elevator repairer normally would not carry. Service crews also do major modernization and alteration work, such as moving and replacing electrical motors, hydraulic pumps, and control panels.

Elevator installers and repairers usually specialize in installation, maintenance, or repair work. Maintenance and repair workers generally need greater knowledge of electricity and electronics than do installers, because a large part of maintenance and repair work is troubleshooting. Similarly, adjusters need a thorough knowledge of electricity, electronics, and computers to ensure that newly installed elevators operate properly.

Training Required

Most elevator installers and repairers apply for their jobs through a local of the International Union of Elevator Constructors; in Canada, an apprenticeship is required. To apply for an apprenticeship position, you must be at least eighteen years old, have a high school diploma or equivalent, and pass an aptitude test. Good physical condition and mechanical aptitude also are important.

You can learn this trade in a program that is administered by local joint educational committees representing the employers and the union. These programs combine on-the-job training with classroom instruction in blueprint reading, electrical and electronic theory, mathematics, applications of physics, and safety—everything from installation to repair. In nonunion shops, you may have the opportunity to take a training program sponsored by independent contractors.

As an apprentice, you must complete a six-month probationary period, after which you'll work toward becoming fully qualified within four years. To be classified as a fully qualified elevator installer or repairer, you will have to pass a standard examination administered by the National Elevator Industry Educational Program. Most states and cities will also require that you pass a licensing examination. Both union and nonunion technicians may take the Certified Elevator Technician or the Certified Accessibility and Private Residence Lift Technician program courses offered by the National Association of Elevator Contractors.

The Canadian Elevator Industry Education Program is a combination of training courses offered by the International Union of Elevator Constructors (IUEC) and working as an apprentice in the elevator industry. For fifty-two weeks you'll work as a probationary helper, earning 55 percent of a mechanic's hourly wage to start. After twenty-six weeks, the rate increases to 60 percent, and you participate in the company pension plan. After fifty-two weeks, you apply to become a member of the union. Then you can start taking IUEC courses. You become recognized at the national level once you have completed this apprenticeship training program, which usually lasts four to five years.

Most apprentices assist experienced elevator installers and repairers. Beginners carry materials and tools, bolt rails to walls, and assemble elevator cars. Eventually, apprentices learn more difficult tasks such as wiring, which requires knowledge of local and national electrical codes.

High school courses in electricity, mathematics, and physics provide a useful background. As elevators become increasingly sophisticated, you may find that you need to acquire more advanced formal education with an emphasis on electronics, perhaps in a postsecondary technical school or junior college. Additional formal education, such as an associate degree, may help you to advance more quickly.

Many elevator installers and repairers also receive training from their employers or through manufacturers to become familiar with a particular company's equipment. Retraining is very important to keep abreast of technological developments in the field. In fact, union elevator installers and repairers typically receive continual training throughout their careers, through correspondence courses, seminars, or formal classes. Although voluntary, this training can greatly improve chances for job security and promotion.

Advancement

Some installers may receive further training in specialized areas and advance to the position of mechanic-in-charge, adjuster, supervisor, or elevator inspector. Adjusters, for example, may be picked for their position because they possess particular skills or are electronically inclined. Other workers may move into management, sales, or product design jobs.

Compensation

Earnings of elevator installers and repairers are among the highest of all construction trades. Median hourly earnings were $28.23 in 2004. The majority earned between $22.96 and $33.68, while the lowest 10 percent earned less than $17.36, and the top 10 percent earned more than $39.65. Median hourly earnings in the miscellaneous special trade contractors industry were $28.68.

Three out of four elevator installers and repairers were members of unions or were covered by a union contract, one of the highest proportions of all occupations. The largest numbers were members of the International Union of Elevator Constructors. In addition to free continuing education, elevator installers and repairers receive basic benefits enjoyed by most other workers.

Job Outlook

You should expect keen competition for entering this occupation, because the jobs have relatively high earnings and good benefits, they involve a significant investment in training, and a large proportion of them are unionized. As a result, workers tend to stay in this occupation for a long time, and few leave and need to be replaced, thus reducing job opportunities. Job prospects should be best for those with postsecondary education in electronics.

Most of the demand for workers will be due to replacements. Additional opportunities will depend on growth in nonresidential construction, such as commercial office buildings and stores that have elevators and escalators. This sector of the construction industry is expected to grow during the decade in response to economic expansion. In addition, the need to continually update and repair old equipment, expand access to the disabled, and install increasingly sophisticated equipment and computerized controls also should add to the demand for elevator installers and repairers. Adding to the demand for elevator installers and repairers is a growing residential market where an increasing number of the elderly require easier access to their homes through stair lifts and residential elevators.

Elevators, escalators, lifts, moving walkways, and related equipment need to be kept in good working condition year-round, so employment of elevator repairers is less affected by economic downturns and seasonality than other construction trades.

There are two additional trades that don't require licensing but that coexist with those that do. One provides support and the other a finished product.

Sheet Metal Workers

Sheet metal workers make, install, and maintain heating, ventilation, and air-conditioning duct systems; roofs; siding; rain gutters; downspouts; skylights; restaurant equipment; outdoor signs; railroad cars; tailgates; customized precision equipment; and many other products made from metal sheets. They also may work with fiberglass and plastic materials. Although some specialize in fabrication, installation, or maintenance, most do all three jobs. Sheet metal workers do both construction-related sheet metal work and mass production of sheet metal products in manufacturing.

At the start of a job, sheet metal workers study plans and specifications to determine the kind and quantity of materials they will need. They measure, cut, bend, shape, and fasten pieces of sheet metal to make ductwork, countertops, and other custom products. In an increasing number of shops, they use computerized metalworking equipment that enables them to perform their tasks more quickly and to experiment with different layouts to find the one that results in the least waste of material. They cut, drill, and form parts with computer-controlled saws, lasers, shears, and presses.

In shops without computerized equipment, and for products that cannot be made on such equipment, sheet metal workers make the required calculations and use tapes, rulers, and other measuring devices for layout work. They then cut or stamp the parts on machine tools.

Before assembling pieces, they check each part for accuracy using measuring instruments such as calipers and micrometers and, if necessary, finish it by using hand, rotary, or squaring shears and hacksaws. After the parts have been inspected, workers fasten seams and joints together with welds, bolts, cement, rivets, solder, specially formed sheet metal drive clips, or other connecting devices. They then take the parts to the construction site, where they further assemble the pieces as they install them. These workers install ducts, pipes, and tubes by joining them end to end and hanging them with metal hangers secured to a ceiling or a wall. They also use shears, hammers, punches, and drills to make parts at the work site or to alter parts made in the shop.

Some jobs are done completely at the job site. When installing a metal roof, for example, workers measure and cut the roofing panels that are needed to complete the job. They secure the first panel in place and interlock and fasten the grooved edge of the next panel into the grooved edge of the first. Then they nail or weld the free edge of the panel to the structure. This two-step process is repeated for each additional panel. Finally, the workers fasten machine-made molding at joints, along corners, and around windows and doors for a neat, finished effect.

In addition to installation work, some sheet metal workers specialize in testing, balancing, adjusting, and servicing existing air-conditioning and ventilation systems to make sure they are functioning properly and to improve their energy efficiency. Because properly installed duct systems are a key component to heating, ventilation, and air-conditioning (HVAC) systems, duct installers are sometimes referred to as HVAC technicians. A growing activity for sheet metal workers is building commissioning, which is a complete mechanical inspection of a building's HVAC, water, and lighting systems.

Workers in manufacturing plants make sheet metal parts for products such as aircraft or industrial equipment. Although some of the fabrication techniques used in large-scale manufacturing are similar to those used in smaller shops, the work may be highly automated and repetitive. Sheet metal workers doing such work may be responsible for reprogramming the computer control systems of the equipment they operate.

Training Required

This trade can be learned through both formal and informal training programs; it usually takes between four and five years of both classroom and on-the-job training. Preparation can begin in high school, where classes in English, algebra, geometry, physics, mechanical drawing and blueprint reading, and general shop are recommended.

After high school, you have a number of options. One is to find a job with a contractor who will provide on-the-job training. You will start as a helper assisting more experienced workers, carrying metal, and cleaning up debris in a metal shop while you learn about materials and tools. Later, you'll learn to operate machines that bend or cut metal. In time, you will go out on job sites to learn installation, and your employer may send you to courses at a trade or vocational school or community college to receive further formal training. Once you've gained sufficient knowledge and skills, you may be promoted to the journeyman level. Most sheet metal workers in large-scale manufacturing receive on-the-job training, with additional class work or in-house training as necessary.

Formal apprenticeships are offered by some employers, particularly large nonresidential construction contractors with union membership. These programs combine on-the-job training with related classroom instruction. Usually, you must be at least eighteen years old and meet local requirements. The length of your program, typically four to five years, varies based on your skill. An apprenticeship program will provide comprehensive instruction in both sheet metal fabrication and installation. Programs may be administered by local joint committees composed of the Sheet Metal Workers' International Association and local chapters of the Sheet Metal and Air-Conditioning Contractors National Association.

As an apprentice, you will learn on the job the basics of pattern layout and how to cut, bend, fabricate, and install sheet metal. You'll begin by learning to install and maintain basic ductwork and gradually advance to more difficult jobs, such as making more complex ducts, commercial kitchens, and decorative pieces. You will also use materials such as fiberglass, plastics, and other nonmetallic materials. Depending on your employer, you may focus on exterior or architectural sheet metal installation. Your classroom studies will include drafting, plan and specification reading, trigonometry and geometry applicable to layout work, the use of computerized equipment, welding, and the principles of heating, air-conditioning, and ventilating systems. Safety is stressed throughout the program. In addition, you'll learn the relationship between sheet metal work and other construction work.

You must be in good physical condition and have mechanical and mathematical aptitude as well as good reading skills to succeed as a sheet metal worker. Good eye-hand coordination, spatial and form perception, and manual dexterity also are important. Courses in algebra, trigonometry, geometry, mechanical drawing, and shop will provide you with a helpful background for learning the trade, as does related work experience obtained in the armed services.

It is important for experienced sheet metal workers to keep abreast of new technological developments, such as the use of computerized layout and laser-cutting machines. Workers often take additional training, provided by the union or by their employer, to improve existing skills or to acquire new ones.

Advancement

Sheet metal workers in construction may advance to supervisory jobs. Some take additional training in welding and do more specialized work. Those who perform building and system testing are able to move into construction and building inspection; others go into the contracting business for themselves. Because a sheet metal contractor must have a shop with equipment to fabricate products, this type of contracting business is more expensive to start than other types of construction contracting. Sheet metal workers in manufacturing may advance to positions as supervisors or quality inspectors. Some of these workers may move into other management positions.

Compensation

In 2004, median hourly earnings of sheet metal workers were approximately $17.09. The middle 50 percent earned between $12.49 and $23.89, while the lowest 10 percent of all sheet metal workers earned less than $9.80, and the highest 10 percent earned more than $30.78.

Apprentices normally start at about 40 percent to 50 percent of the rate paid to experienced workers. They receive periodic pay raises as they acquire more skills, until their pay approaches that of experienced workers. In addition, union workers in some areas receive supplemental wages from the union when they are on lay-off or shortened workweeks.

Job Outlook

Job opportunities are expected to be good for sheet metal workers in the construction industry, reflecting both employment growth and openings arising each year as experienced workers leave the occupation. Opportunities should be particularly good for those with apprenticeship training or who are certified welders. Prospects in manufacturing will not be as good because a number of manufacturing plants that employ sheet metal workers are moving to parts of the country or abroad where the wages are lower, and the ones that remain are becoming more productive.

Employment of sheet metal workers is expected to reflect growth in the number of industrial, commercial, and residential structures being built. The need to install energy-efficient air-conditioning, heating, and ventilation systems in older buildings as well as to perform other types of renovation and maintenance work should also boost employment. In addition, the popularity of decorative sheet metal products and increased architectural restoration are expected to add to demand.

Sheet metal workers in construction may experience periods of unemployment, particularly when construction projects end and economic conditions dampen activity. Nevertheless, employment in this trade is less sensitive to declines in new construction than is the employment of other construction workers, such as carpenters.

Maintenance of existing equipment makes up a large part of the work that is done by sheet metal workers. Installation of new air-conditioning and heating systems in existing buildings continues during construction slumps, as individuals and businesses adopt more energy-efficient equipment to cut utility bills. In addition, a large proportion of sheet metal installation and maintenance is done indoors, so workers usually lose less work time due to bad weather than other construction workers do.

Heating, Air-Conditioning, and Refrigeration Mechanics and Installers

Heating and air-conditioning systems control the temperature, humidity, and total air quality in all types of buildings. Refrigeration systems make it possible to store and transport food, medicine, and other perishable items. Both types of systems are installed, maintained, and repaired by heating, air-conditioning, and refrigeration mechanics and installers, who are also called *technicians*. Because heating, ventilation, air-conditioning, and refrigeration systems often are referred to as HVACR systems, these workers are often called *HVACR technicians*.

HVACR consists of many mechanical, electrical, and electronic components, such as motors, compressors, pumps, fans, ducts, pipes, thermostats, and switches. For example, in central forced-air heating systems, a furnace heats air that is distributed throughout the building through a system of metal or fiberglass ducts. Technicians must be able to maintain, diagnose, and correct problems throughout the entire system. They accomplish this by adjusting system controls to recommended settings and testing the performance of the entire system using special tools and test equipment.

Technicians often specialize in installation or maintenance and repair, although they are trained to do both. They also may specialize in doing heating work or air-conditioning or refrigeration work. Some work with one type of equipment, such as *hydronics* (water-based heating systems), solar panels, or commercial refrigeration. Technicians also try to sell their clients service contracts that provide for regular maintenance of the heating and cooling systems and help to reduce the seasonal fluctuations of this type of work.

HVACR technicians follow blueprints or other specifications to install oil, gas, electric, solid-fuel, and multiple-fuel heating systems and air-conditioning systems. After putting the equipment in place, they install fuel and water supply lines, air ducts and vents, pumps, and other components. They may connect electrical wiring and controls and check the unit for proper operation. To ensure the proper functioning of the system, furnace installers often use combustion test equipment, such as carbon dioxide testers, carbon monoxide testers, combustion analyzers, and oxygen testers.

After a furnace or air-conditioning unit has been installed, technicians perform routine maintenance and repair work to keep the systems operating efficiently. They may adjust burners and blowers and check for leaks. If the system is not operating properly, they check the thermostat, burner nozzles, controls, or other parts to diagnose and then correct the problem.

Technicians perform maintenance work during the summer, when the heating system is not in use, which includes replacing filters, ducts, and other parts of the system that may accumulate dust and impurities during the operating season. During the winter, air-conditioning mechanics inspect the systems and do required maintenance, such as overhauling compressors.

Refrigeration mechanics install, service, and repair industrial and commercial refrigerating systems and a variety of refrigeration equipment. They follow blueprints, design specifications, and manufacturers' instructions to install motors, compressors, condensing units, evaporators, piping, and other components. They connect this equipment to the ductwork, refrigerant lines, and electrical power source. After making the connections, they charge the system with refrigerant, check it for proper operation, and program control systems.

When air-conditioning and refrigeration technicians service equipment, they must use care to conserve, recover, and recycle chlorofluorocarbon (CFC), hydrochlorofluorocarbon (HCFC), hydrofluorocarbon (HFC), and other refrigerants used in these systems, because the release of these refrigerants can be harmful to the environment. They conserve the refrigerant by making sure that there are no leaks in the system and recover it by venting the refrigerant into proper cylinders. They then recycle it for reuse with special filter-dryers or ensure that it is properly disposed.

HVACR mechanics and installers are adept at using a variety of tools, including hammers, wrenches, metal snips, electric drills, pipe cutters and benders, measurement gauges, and acetylene torches, to work with refrigerant lines and air ducts. They use voltmeters, thermometers, pressure gauges, manometers, and other testing devices to check airflow, refrigerant pressure, electrical circuits, burners, and other components.

Training Required

Because of the increasing sophistication of air-conditioning, refrigeration, and heating systems, employers prefer to hire workers with technical school training or those who have completed an apprenticeship. However, some mechanics and installers still learn the trade informally on the job.

You can find six-month to two-year programs in heating, air-conditioning, and refrigeration at many secondary and postsecondary technical and trade schools, junior and community colleges, and with the U.S. Armed Forces. Your studies will include theory, design, and equipment construction, as well as electronics, and you will learn the basics of installation, maintenance, and repair. There are three accrediting agencies that have set academic standards for HVACR programs: HVAC Excellence, the National Center for Construction Education and Research, and the Partnership for Air Conditioning, Heating, and Refrigeration Accreditation. After completing these programs, new technicians generally need between an additional six months and two years of field experience before they can be considered proficient.

Apprenticeship programs frequently are run by joint committees representing local chapters of the Air-Conditioning Contractors of America, the Mechanical Contractors Association of America, Plumbing-Heating-Cooling Contractors–National Association, and locals of the Sheet Metal Workers' International Association or the United Association of Journeymen and Apprentices of the Plumbing and Pipefitting Industry of the United States and Canada. Other apprenticeship programs are sponsored by local chapters of the Associated Builders and Contractors and the National Association of Home Builders. Formal apprenticeship programs normally last three to five years and combine on-the-job training with classroom instruction. Classes include subjects such as the use and care of tools, safety practices, blueprint reading, and the theory and design of heating, ventilation, air-conditioning, and refrigeration systems. You must have a high school diploma or equivalent to apply for these programs, and math and reading skills are essential. After completing an apprenticeship program, you will be considered a skilled technician capable of working alone. These programs are also a pathway to certification and in some cases college credits.

If you choose to acquire your skills on the job, you'll most likely begin by assisting experienced technicians, perhaps performing simple tasks such as carrying materials, insulating refrigerant lines, or cleaning furnaces. In time, you'll move on to more difficult tasks, such as cutting and soldering pipes and sheet metal and checking electrical and electronic circuits.

Courses in shop math, mechanical drawing, applied physics and chemistry, electronics, blueprint reading, and computer applications will provide a good background. Some knowledge of plumbing or electrical work is also helpful, and a basic understanding of electronics is becoming more important because of the increasing use of this technology in equipment controls. Because technicians frequently deal directly with the public, you should be courteous and tactful, especially when dealing with an aggravated customer. You should be in good physical condition because technicians sometimes have to lift and move heavy equipment.

All technicians who purchase or work with refrigerants must be certified in their proper handling. To become certified to purchase and handle refrigerants, you must pass a written examination specific to the type of work in which you will specialize. The three possible areas of certification are Type I, servicing small appliances; Type II, high-pressure refrigerants; and Type III, low-pressure refrigerants. Exams are administered by organizations approved by the U.S. Environmental Protection Agency and Environment Canada, such as trade schools, unions, contractor associations, or building groups.

Throughout the learning process, you may have to take a number of tests that measure your skills in the field. For those with less than one year of experience and who are taking classes, the industry has developed a series of exams to test basic competency in residential heating and cooling, light commercial heating and cooling, and commercial refrigeration. These entry-level certification exams are commonly conducted at both secondary and postsecondary technical and trade schools. For HVACR technicians who have at least one year of experience performing installations and two years of experience performing maintenance and repair, there are a number of different tests to certify their competency in working with more specific types of equipment, such as oil-burning furnaces. The tests are offered through Refrigeration Service Engineers Society, HVAC Excellence, the Carbon Monoxide Safety Association, Air Conditioning and Refrigeration Safety Coalition, and North American Technician Excellence, Inc., among others. Passing these tests and obtaining certification is increasingly recommended by employers and may increase advancement opportunities.

Advancement

Advancement usually takes the form of higher pay. However, some technicians may advance to positions as supervisor or service manager. Others may move into areas such as sales and marketing. Still others may become building superintendents, cost estimators, or, with the necessary certification, teachers. Those who have sufficient money and managerial skill can open their own contracting business.

Compensation

Median hourly earnings of heating, air-conditioning, and refrigeration mechanics and installers were $17.43 in 2004. Most earned between $13.51 and $22.21 an hour, but the lowest 10 percent earned less than $10.88, and the top 10 percent earned more than $27.11.

Apprentices usually begin at about 50 percent of the wage rate paid to experienced workers. As they gain experience and improve their skills, they receive periodic increases until they reach the wage rate of experienced workers.

Heating, air-conditioning, and refrigeration mechanics and installers enjoy a variety of employer-sponsored benefits. In addition to typical benefits such as health insurance and pension plans, some employers pay for work-related training and provide uniforms, company vans, and tools.

About 16 percent of HVACR mechanics and installers are members of a union. The unions to which the greatest numbers of mechanics and installers belong are the Sheet Metal Workers International Association and the United Association of Journeymen and Apprentices of the Plumbing and Pipefitting Industry of the United States and Canada.

Job Outlook

Job prospects in this trade are expected to be excellent—particularly for those who have training from an accredited technical school or who have formal apprenticeship training—especially in the fastest-growing areas of the country. A growing number of retirements of highly skilled technicians are expected to generate many job openings. In addition, employment is projected to increase between 18 percent and 26 percent through 2014.

As the population and stock of buildings grow, so does the demand for residential, commercial, and industrial climate-control systems. The increased complexity of HVACR systems, increasing the possibility that equipment may malfunction, also will create opportunities for service technicians. Technicians who specialize in installation work may experience periods of unemployment when the level of new construction activity declines, but maintenance and repair work usually remain relatively stable. People and businesses depend on their climate-control systems and must keep them in good working order, regardless of economic conditions.

Concern for the environment has prompted the development of new energy-saving heating and air-conditioning systems. An emphasis on better energy management should lead to the replacement of older systems and the installation of newer, more efficient systems in existing homes and buildings. Also, demand for maintenance and service work should increase as businesses and home owners strive to keep increasingly complex systems operating at peak efficiency. Regulations prohibiting the discharge and production of CFC and HCFC refrigerants should continue to result in the need to replace many existing air-conditioning systems or modify them to use new environmentally safe refrigerants.

A growing focus on improving indoor air quality, as well as the increasing use of refrigerated equipment by a growing number of stores and gasoline stations that sell food, also should contribute to the creation of more jobs for heating, air-conditioning, and refrigeration technicians.

A Final Word

Working in sheet metal or HVACR can provide you with many opportunities in building construction. As you have seen, these two trades form the basis for others and are in high demand.

Although the need for licensing adds an additional step to your training process, it is genuinely worthwhile if you wish to advance as an electrician, plumber, or elevator installer. Many people spend their entire careers in these trades. However, they cannot advance to a fully qualified tradesperson. Don't be afraid of the additional training; it will only benefit you in the end.

7

CONTRACTORS, BUILDERS, AND REMODELERS

IF CONSTRUCTION IS the assembly of many parts into a finished building, then the central figures in the industry are those who put these parts together. The builders, the contractors, the factory assemblers, and their dealers are the professionals who are responsible for organizing a construction project. They may correctly be called *entrepreneurs*, a word that aptly describes today's builder as a person who organizes and manages a business undertaking, assuming the risk in order to make a profit.

Any work on a new building entails many steps before actual construction begins. It requires preparation of land, development of a master plan, providing utilities, laying out streets, and, finally, erection of the structure.

The entrepreneur must be both a businessperson and a merchant. Unless a building is being constructed on contract for someone else, it must either be sold or rented while it is being built or after completion. It must provide sufficient profit to sustain the builder's future projects, or it must provide enough repetitive income in the way of rental money to sustain operations.

The builder-entrepreneur is, in most cases, representative of one of the last "free" professions. The industry itself imposes no licensing or educational restrictions. All that is needed to enter the profession of home building is knowledge of construction, some aptitude for business, working capital, and a large capacity for hard and long work.

There are two basic types of organizations in the construction industry, the builder and the general contractor. A builder generally is responsible for all of the functions of a project, such as purchasing and developing land, design, acquisition of construction money and final mortgage loans, and construction of the building. Finally, builders take care of the disposition or sale of the unit or may hold it for themselves as investment, collecting income from it.

General contractors usually build with someone else's money. They are not responsible for disposition of the property; in most cases, their only function is to build the structure. They coordinate the project, taking full responsibility for the complete job, except for specified portions of the work that may be omitted from the general contract. Although general contractors may do a portion of the work with their own crews, they often subcontract most of the work to heavy construction or specialty trade contractors.

Specialty trade contractors usually do the work of only one trade, such as painting, carpentry, or electrical work, or of two or more closely related trades, such as plumbing and heating. Beyond fitting their work to that of the other trades, they have no responsibility for the structure as a whole and obtain orders for their work from general contractors, architects, or property owners. Repair work is almost always done on direct order from owners, occupants, architects, or rental agents. When hired by a general contractor, specialty trade contractors are called *subcontractors*.

Considering the number of builders, general contractors, and trades, you can see that the construction industry is made up of literally hundreds of business entities, small and specialized. For this reason, the housing industry does not have well-defined boundaries, and many building and contracting firms are involved in other activities in addition to construction. Many home builders are also involved in the land development business, some are real estate brokers, and others devote a good part of their business to commercial and remodeling work and even insurance. So entrepreneurs who are ambitious and smart businesspeople can combine building homes with other business opportunities to create a fulfilling career that includes steady work and different challenges. For example, a contractor who works primarily in school construction, which is mostly done during the summer months, can spend the winter season building a house. This keeps the business active all year and allows the builder to combine two profitable activities.

Entrepreneur

The construction industry provides a tremendous number of opportunities for workers to advance and own their own businesses. As you've already read about, there are many construction trades, and workers in all of them have opened their own companies. A contributing factor to the ease with which construction workers can become entrepreneurs is the industry's comparatively low requirements of capital, plant and office space, and full-time personnel. However, though it may be fairly easy to start a construction business, the work involves much risk, and the failure rate is high in comparison to most other industries. The move from salaried or wage employee in the construction industry to private entrepreneurship takes many forms. Many workers in the building trades move into contracting from jobs as foremen and construction superintendents. Some get their start working in clerical or administrative positions in a contractor's office, where they are given an opportunity to learn estimating and purchasing. A small, growing, and important number start with college training in architecture, engineering, building construction, and business administration.

Home Builder

Because residential construction accounts for annual expenditures of more than $4 billion, the public tends to associate a home builder with big business. However, the typical home builder is nothing of the sort. Most are small entrepreneurs building only a handful of houses each year. According to a survey by the National Association of Home Builders, the average number of units built by an individual builder is fewer than twenty a year.

There is also a popular belief that the large builders are going to become larger, and the small-custom or small-tract builder is going to vanish. However, the opposite seems to be true, and there are some very good reasons for this.

The nature of the housing market itself favors the small builder. There is no national market, only local markets spread throughout thousands of communities. These local markets are as individual as the communities themselves, and what is selling in one will not necessarily sell even a few miles away. Taste and wants in housing are as individual as clothing styles.

With that said, however, the success of large custom-building companies cannot be overlooked. Some large merchant builders have the capability to complete several thousand units a year in various locations. Toll Brothers, for example, has grown into a Fortune 500 company that builds in twenty-two states, constructing luxury homes and estates, adult communities, condominiums, and golf communities. In 2006, the average price of a completed home was $690,000. While this is certainly not the average home builder, it is an example of how vast the market is and the kinds of opportunities that exist in the industry.

In general, the building industry is much more competitive now than it was after World War II. There are only a few Levittowns— huge, low-priced housing projects—in the country. One reason is that this type of operation was possible after the great housing drought during the Depression of the 1930s and during World War II. When the GIs returned and started families, a tremendous need for shelter had to be satisfied. After this was accomplished, a more selective customer appeared and demanded more than just a shelter. As the nation grew even more prosperous, the median sales price of new homes rose. Families demanded more space, more household comforts, and more facilities.

One of the reasons small builders do so well is that they are able to operate with lower overhead than big builders. In most cases they are the supervisors, and many even act as their own carpenters. Designs and plans—basic in themselves—are altered, changed, and made more sophisticated at little cost but are intended to appeal to the particular community in which a building is being constructed.

The progress in construction methods over the years has been evolutionary rather than revolutionary, and while higher and higher orders of technology are being introduced into the business—new materials, components, and methods of land planning—the basics remain little changed.

Building continues to be a major component of free enterprise in the United States and Canada. The mechanics of the economic system, with individual drives, desires, and ingenuity, make it possible to succeed in the building marketplace and make it advantageous to enter this field.

A Changing Industry

Perhaps one of the most significant trends in the construction industry in recent years has been the diversification of activities by builders. This diversification is in direct response to the changing nature of the construction industry. The striking changes in the volume of builders' production of units caused by rapid changes in interest rates forced and encouraged builders to enter many different fields of construction activity rather than restricting themselves to one type of activity. For example, the percentages have shifted from more speculative builders and fewer remodelers to an increasing number of remodeling firms and a lower percentage of builders working on speculation.

So, for the person who is considering a career in the building construction trades, opportunities abound in small-, medium-, and large-sized firms. All have their own advantages and disadvantages. Working for a small builder presents the opportunity to be involved in all phases of the operation. Employment with a large builder, on the other hand, is similar to working for a corporation, with all the advantages of benefits and the chance to diversify into different types of work.

Generally, home builders in this industry may be placed in three broad categories: the speculative builder, the custom builder, and the remodeling builder. Remodeling is an increasingly important part of the industry that will be considered as a separate item later in this chapter.

Speculative Builder

Most builders enter this field by building a single house for sale. The builder may already own a piece of ground or may have to buy land. In the latter case, the builder will either have to pay cash for the land or negotiate terms. It is not unusual to obtain favorable terms or even to persuade a seller to take a note for some part or the whole amount of land value, contingent on the note's being repaid after the house is sold.

A building lot should represent no more than about 25 percent to 33 percent of the final sale price of the land and the house that the builder intends to construct. To put it another way, if the intended sales price of a home is going to be $250,000, the cash needed for the developed lot should be about $62,500 to $82,500.

With the land acquired, a prospective builder normally goes to a financial institution, such as a commercial bank or credit union, to apply for a construction loan. The builder must have a set of plans to show what kind of house will be built, a financial statement, and a market analysis that will show that there is indeed a market for such houses at such a location. The builder then shows how and when he or she intends to repay the loan.

The builder can probably count on receiving at least 50 percent of the intended sales price in a construction loan. Let's take the intended sales price of $250,000 as an example. The builder already has paid $62,500 for the lot. The builder will now be able to draw against the construction loan approximately $125,000; however, this will not be enough to complete the house. The builder is counting on making a net profit of 15 percent before taxes, and this will be calculated as a percentage of the final price of $250,000. The builder is hoping, therefore, to make about $37,500 net. The land and construction loan will provide $187,500, but $212,500 ($250,000 less the $37,500 profit) will be needed to complete the house. Thus the builder still needs $25,000 to complete the house.

This $25,000 line of credit may be borrowed at a commercial bank, but in choosing this option the builder is taking the chance that the house will sell quickly. This may happen, and then again, it may not. The downturns in the real estate market that began in late 2006 left many houses vacant for much longer than builders anticipated, causing many to exceed their initial financial plans. For this reason, it's a better idea to have the additional money needed to complete the project available rather than borrow it.

This example illustrates two points. One is that it does not really take a large investment to start in home building. The second is that to be successful, a prospective entrepreneur needs about one-third of the sales price in cash (unless the land is already paid for).

Of course, a large speculative builder is a different type of individual from those who are just trying their wings in building their first houses. Better described as a merchant builder, a large builder might build more than one hundred houses a year. A volume of one hundred units at an average 2007 sales price of $250,000 would mean an annual volume of about $25 million.

While a small builder can usually operate with little administrative support and a good record-keeping system, a reasonably large merchant builder will organize the business into various departments, such as accounting, finance (mortgages), marketing (sales), construction, and administrative.

Custom Builder

A custom builder is exactly what it sounds like—someone who builds on order from customers. The custom builder is contacted by individuals or by companies to submit a price for a certain building job, which can be a house or any other kind of construction in which the builder specializes. Usually the builder will receive plans from a potential client, make the estimates of costs, and submit this estimate to the client in one price.

While this kind of operation can be highly lucrative, it does have its pitfalls and aggravations. Frequent demands by the client for changes during construction may erode a substantial part of the builder's profits. Unless the builder is strong enough to withstand repeated requests by the buyer (which many times is impossible to do), all the projected costs may change drastically. Prospective home builders are well advised not to get into custom contract construction unless they are able to have a very specific understanding of what the end product is to be, what quality of materials and labor they are to provide, and the limits placed, contractually, on the kinds of changes that may be permitted.

Remodeling Industry

Remodeling is a booming section of building construction, and it provides great opportunities for people who are considering construction careers.

The industry is growing for a number of reasons. Many home owners choose to remodel or completely renovate their existing homes rather than spend the money to purchase a new home. In communities where the majority of homes are small bungalow types that were once seasonal residences, buyers are renovating these houses to add more bedrooms, an extra bath, and modern kitchen. As the baby boomer generation ages, more people are choosing to renovate their current homes to accommodate their changing needs; this option is also becoming popular among people who bring an elderly parent or relative into their homes.

As of the third quarter of 2006, there were 126,225,000 homes in the United States. Given this number, the possibilities for remodelers are many. And while there are certainly a number of large remodeling firms that employ full staffs of craftworkers and even architects and designers, this field is an excellent place for the small contractor to find success. According to the U.S. Census of Construction, of the 82,750 remodeling establishments operating in 2002, only 64,946 had fewer than five employees.

Types of Remodeling Jobs

The types of jobs covered under remodeling are broadly classified as either maintenance and repairs or construction improvements. Improvements are further classified as additions to residential buildings, alterations within residential buildings, additions and alterations on property outside the residential buildings, and major replacements.

Maintenance and repair jobs include painting, papering, floor sanding, and furnace cleaning or adjustment. Repairs include many kinds of expenditures for plumbing, heating, electrical work, and other kinds of activity involved in the upkeep of homes. Repairs also include replacement of parts. For example, roof repairs (including replacement of shingles and gutters) are classified under maintenance and repairs, but a complete roofing job is classified as a major replacement. Plumbing repairs may include extensive replacement of water pipes, but if the entire piping system is removed and a new one put in, the work is considered a major replacement.

Construction improvements cover work that is considered a capital investment in the property. These include additions to residential homes, alterations to homes, additions and alterations on property outside the home, and major replacements. Additions to residential homes refer to the actual enlargement of the structure by adding a wing, room, porch, attached garage, shed, or carport or by raising the roof or digging a basement. Additions within residential homes include changes or improvements made within or on the building. They can range from a complete remodeling, which involves removal and renovation of the entire inside of the home, to the installation of a new electric service outlet, new wall switch, or new shelf.

Additions and alterations on the property outside the home include laying or improving walks or driveways; building walls or fences; creating or improving recreational facilities, such as swimming pools, tennis courts, and barbeque facilities; and building detached garages, sheds, patios, or greenhouses or the improvement of these.

Major replacements that are classified as construction improvements are confined to the following list of large individual items.

- Complete furnace or boiler
- Entire roof
- Central air conditioner
- All siding
- Water heater
- Entire electrical wiring system

- Bathtub or shower
- All water pipes
- Washbasin
- Septic tank or cesspool
- Toilet
- Complete walks or driveways
- Sink or laundry tub
- Kitchen cabinets
- Garbage disposal unit

Growth of Remodeling

The amount of money spent on remodeling activities has grown tremendously over the past forty years. Beginning in 1967 (the first year the U.S. Department of Commerce began keeping statistics on this type of activity), the industry spent only $11.7 billion on remodeling. This number is expected to reach $250 billion in 2007. Coming off the strongest five years in its history, the remodeling market is expected to maintain its momentum, with a growth rate of 5 percent each year through 2016.

Professionals in the industry reinforce this positive outlook. "The last five years were probably the best five years in remodeling history," said Kermit Baker, the director of the Remodeling Futures Program of Harvard's Joint Center for Housing Studies. "There was growing equity and low interest rates. All the forces came together. It was the perfect storm for remodeling. But we are seeing the tide turning a little." A slowdown in home construction usually means less spending on additions and alterations. However, maintenance and repairs help buoy the remodeling market. "Remodeling is less cyclical than new construction," Baker noted.

"When someone has a leaky roof, they have no choice but to fix it," added Gopal Ahluwalia, the National Association of Home Builder's vice president of research, who has pioneered studies of the remodeling market for the past twenty years. "Maintenance and repairs will not be affected." Home owners tend to customize their homes several years after they purchase, and more than thirty million homes sold in the past five years should continue to feed the remodeling market for several more years, "unless interest rates rise above 7.5 percent," Ahluwalia said.

According to Kermit Baker, remodelers are the most fragmented of the residential industry players, and he does not foresee major consolidation of the industry in the future. According to his findings, the number of self-employed contractors, both general and special trade, increased faster between 1997 and 2002 than larger firms with payrolls and employees. During those five years, the number of remodeling firms grew from a little more than 400,000 firms to 520,000 firms. He said that industry consolidation is not as feasible because remodeling requires customer-specific custom work that cannot be duplicated on a large scale.

Business Organization

Whether a builder works in speculation, custom work, or remodeling, the company will need to adhere to one of the three primary types of business organizations. These are sole proprietorship, corporation, and partnership. A small builder can choose among them to find the best option, but each should be considered carefully before making a decision.

Many small builders are sole proprietors, operating without any formal type of business organization. The main advantage of sole proprietorship is the simplicity of organization and the low overhead or cost of operation. It is usually most practical when the company and operation are small and can be run efficiently by a single individual. The greatest disadvantage is liability. A sole proprietor usually is liable for the operation and product with everything he or she possesses, meaning that all of the business owner's personal assets are vulnerable in the event of a lawsuit or other financial problem.

A simple form of corporation would limit the owners' liability to only that amount that is in the corporation. Moreover, the tax benefits of a corporation permit the owners to make more profits. By setting up more than one corporation for the whole construction process, for instance, and limiting profits to below a certain amount in each corporation, tax benefits can be achieved that might not accrue to a sole proprietor.

A corporation is best used when sales volume reaches about $1.5 million and more annually. Operating and administrative functions at this volume must be compartmentalized, because it is virtually impossible for one person to run the whole business. Further, the risk of liability gets to be too high for a single individual to assume.

A partnership may be the best vehicle when two or more people combine individual skills for their common good. Many times one person is unable to cope with all of the technical, administrative, and financial problems, and a partnership arrangement needs diverse and specialized talents for efficient operation. However, it is a very good idea to make a partnership a legal matter to protect all parties. Too many people enter into partnerships with friends believing that nothing will come between them. Unfortunately, they later find that they disagree about important business issues and often the partnership cannot withstand the pressure. In these cases, all partners lose.

Management Factors

There are certain basic functions that any builder, small or large, must exercise. These can be summed up as follows:

• **Management function.** A builder must be able to get along with people, whether they are employees, clients, or other tradespeople working on the job.

• **Cost function.** A builder must know the value and meaning of time and its cost and be able to operate in the most efficient and profitable way possible.

• **Construction function.** A builder or a manager of a team must be a businessperson who understands land factors, cost development, and use of land; who knows how to construct units; who is a designer, understanding at least the fundamentals of good design; who knows how to market the product and understands the needs of the particular area in which he or she has selected to build; who is an administrator, able to manage what often may be a very complex organization; and who is a financier, knowing when and how to borrow at the lowest cost, when to repay, and when to invest.

There are other prerequisites, some tangible, others based on the capacity to take risks judiciously and to work hard. They include:

• **Integrity.** This means being honest with yourself, your associates, your employees, and your customers. A good reputation is the finest asset you can have in the home-building business.

• **Experience.** Any background you have in the business through previous employment or vocational or college study and technical knowledge of construction will be useful. "Luck" is a negligible factor in home building.

- **Drive.** You need to have ambition to succeed.
- **Coolheadedness.** This is the quality of being able to work with people in what can be a daily crisis business.

Administration

As in other business activities, the construction industry requires many disciplines. The entrepreneur parcels his or her functions according to the size of the operation. In general, the first area where a small operation started by one person will show growth is in administration. One of the first employees a builder will need is someone to keep the books, a task that may be delegated to a secretary or to an outside bookkeeping agency or accountant. Then, as the operation grows, a builder may take on a full-time employee, perhaps a bookkeeper, who not only can keep the accounts but also can act as treasurer or even handle cost-estimating and loan applications. Business software packages make it much easier for small companies to manage all these tasks. In many small offices, one administrative assistant can use an industry-specific program that streamlines accounts, billing, customer jobs, and even personnel.

A Final Word

Woodrow Wilson was the first to publicly recognize the construction industry's national importance, so much so that he called for a partner with which the government could plan and put into effect programs that would help further the industry in the United States. Since that time, and despite upturns and downturns, the construction industry has proved itself to be a necessary and enduring part of our lives.

If you aspire to be a contractor, builder, or remodeler, you already have the tools to make this dream come true. As you have seen not only in this chapter but throughout the book, the career possibilities in this industry are many. The right training and experience will shape and mold you into the skilled tradesperson or business owner that you wish to be.

8

Issues and Trends

You now know that construction is one of the largest industries and offers opportunities among its many trades for people with various levels of skill and training. In light of its broad scope, it is not surprising that there are some issues that affect certain aspects of the industry. In addition, a number of trends are emerging that point toward the future of building construction.

Safety

Perhaps the most important issue concerning the construction industry is safety. This is quite logical when you consider the number of construction activities that are carried out in difficult working conditions, using tools and materials that can cause injury and even death if not used properly. To ensure the safety of workers, the federal governments of the United States and Canada have implemented laws regulating several aspects of the industry.

The U.S. Occupational Safety and Health Administration (OSHA) and the Canadian Centre for Occupational Health and Safety (CCOHS) strive to eliminate work-related injuries and illnesses and to ensure the safety of all workers. For the construction industry, both agencies have implemented regulations and directives that cover all aspects of the work.

The following are some of the primary areas regulated by OSHA and CCOHS:

- Asbestos
- Highway work zones
- Asphalt fumes
- Laser hazards
- Confined spaces
- Lead
- Crane, derrick, and hoist safety
- Motor vehicle safety
- Demolition
- Noise and hearing conservation
- Electrical
- Personal protective equipment
- Ergonomics
- Power tools
- Fall protection
- Scaffolding
- Fire safety
- Steel erection
- Hand and power tools
- Trenching and excavation
- Hazardous and toxic substances
- Welding, cutting, and brazing

As an example of how these areas are regulated, let's take a look at OSHA regulations regarding asbestos and lead. In the past, asbestos was widely used in construction, primarily because of its high rate of heat resistance, to fireproof roofing and flooring and for heat insulation. Embedded in materials, asbestos is fairly harmless; airborne, however, it can cause several lung diseases, including lung cancer and asbestosis. Similarly, lead was a common building component found in paint and plumbing fixtures and pipes until the late 1970s. Because it is easily absorbed into the bloodstream, often from breathing lead dust or from eating chips of paint containing lead, it can cause serious health risks, especially in children.

According to OSHA, lead overexposure is one of the most common overexposures found in industry and is a leading cause of workplace illness. In addition, approximately 1.3 million workers currently employed in construction and general industry are exposed to asbestos on the job; the majority of this exposure occurs during the removal of asbestos in renovations and demolition. Controlling exposure can be accomplished through engineering controls, such as isolating the source and using ventilation systems; administrative actions, including limiting workers' exposure time and providing showers; and personal protective equipment such as proper respiratory protection and clothing. Under OSHA regulations, employers are required to provide a training program for all employees exposed to airborne asbestos.

Asbestos and Lead Abatement

Although asbestos and lead are rarely used in buildings today, they must be removed from existing structures due to the dangerous health risks that they pose. This work is done by abatement workers, who remove asbestos, lead, and other hazardous materials from buildings scheduled to be renovated or demolished.

Using a variety of hand and power tools, such as vacuums and scrapers, these workers remove the asbestos and lead from surfaces. A typical residential lead abatement project involves the use of a chemical to strip the lead-based paint from the walls of the home. Abatement workers apply the compound with a putty knife and allow it to dry; then they scrape the hazardous material into an impregnable container for transport and storage. They also use sandblasters and high-pressure water sprayers to remove lead from large structures.

The vacuums utilized by asbestos abatement workers have special, highly efficient filters designed to trap the asbestos until it can be disposed of. During the abatement, special monitors measure the amount of asbestos and lead in the air to protect the workers; in addition, lead abatement workers wear a personal air monitor that indicates the amount of lead to which a worker has been exposed. They also use monitoring devices to identify the asbestos, lead, and other materials that need to be removed from the surfaces of walls and structures.

To minimize any danger to workers, asbestos and lead abatement work is done in a highly structured environment. Each phase of a project is planned in advance, and workers are trained to deal with safety breaches and hazardous situations. Crews and supervisors take every precaution to ensure that the work site is safe. The work can be uncomfortable because of the need to stand, stoop, and kneel for long periods. Some workers must wear fully enclosed personal protective suits for several hours at a time; these suits may be hot and uncomfortable and may even cause some people to experience claustrophobia.

Although there are no formal educational requirements for asbestos and lead abatement work, federal regulations require that workers be licensed. Most employers provide technical training on the job, but a formal thirty-two- to forty-hour training program must be completed to obtain a license. The program covers health hazards, personal protective equipment and clothing, site safety, recognition and identification of hazards, and decontamination. In some cases, workers discover one hazardous material while abating another. If they are not licensed to work with the newly discovered material, they cannot continue to work with it. Many experienced workers opt to take courses in additional disciplines to avoid this situation, which also gives them more employment opportunities than those with a single license.

This is just one example of the many ways that OSHA and CCOHS protect workers. From the ubiquitous hard hat to precautions unseen by the public, the safety of construction workers is of paramount importance.

Injuries and Fatalities

Despite the best efforts of governments and employers, a certain number of injuries, illnesses, and fatalities do occur on construction projects. According to the U.S. Bureau of Labor Statistics, of the 5,702 fatal workplace accidents that occurred in 2005, the highest number, 1,186, were in the construction industry. Slightly more than sixty thousand workers were affected by nonfatal work-related injuries or illnesses, a number that is down significantly from 2004 statistics.

It is vitally important for workers in all building construction trades to observe posted regulations and to follow common sense regarding their safety. Inattention to safety regulations can affect both the workers and the project as a whole.

Women in Construction

Nearly nine hundred thousand women work in construction today, up from six hundred thousand ten years ago. Twenty-five percent of women work for residential building contractors, 12 percent for nonresidential contractors, 1 percent for heavy construction and highway contractors, and 62 percent for specialty trade contractors.

Women not only work in construction, they are also moving into management and ownership. Of the 7.5 million businesses owned by women in 2006, 11 percent were in construction. Although this is below the one-third of women-owned businesses for all industries, the construction companies owned by women had higher average revenues ($386 million) than did all other construction firms ($298 million).

Issues Faced by Women

Although it is unfortunate, many women in construction must deal with sexism in this male-dominated industry. There are many underlying causes for sexist attitudes, and women must find a way to handle the negative comments and behaviors of their bosses, coworkers, and even their employees.

There isn't any one way of confronting sexism, and the response might vary depending on a woman's position in the company and her relationship to the perpetrator. For instance, many women who are harassed by coworkers report that they have tried ignoring the sexism, shouting, responding in kind, or threatening legal action. One woman reported trying all of these tactics until she learned to stop worrying about whether her coworkers liked her. Once she stopped trying to fit in and developed a more confident attitude, coworkers began to tire of bothering her.

Women in management or ownership positions have to deal carefully with this issue. Even though a woman is the boss, she may still face insubordination from male workers. One woman reports that once she developed confidence, she was able to say, "You work for me. If you can't follow my rules, find another job."

The female vice president and sales manager of a remodeling firm says she is careful not to use her construction knowledge as a way to prove herself, because it can make people feel that she's challenging them. The female president of a custom building firm says that a good deal of workplace prejudice is more the result of class than gender. Because her background is in academics rather than construction, she had to work hard to learn the language of the trades. Once she did this, crews responded much more positively because they no longer felt that she was condescending to them.

To strengthen their position and gain a voice in this very much male-dominated industry, women have banded together to form professional organizations through which they can continue to learn and help one another achieve success.

National Association of Women in Construction

The National Association of Women in Construction (NAWIC) originally began as Women in Construction of Fort Worth, Texas. It was founded in 1953 by sixteen women working in the construction industry as a support network for the small number of women in the field. The organization was so successful that it gained its national charter in 1955 and became the National Association of Women in Construction.

The core purpose of NAWIC is to enhance the success of women in the construction industry. To help achieve its goal, the organization has established *The NAWIC Image*, its official publication. In addition, the NAWIC Founders Scholarship Foundation (NFSF) awards scholarships to students pursuing construction-related studies, and the NAWIC Education Foundation (NEF) develops programs for children and adults.

Today NAWIC is an international nonprofit organization with a membership of fifty-five hundred women in 179 chapters in nearly every U.S. state. In 2006 it signed an International Affiliation Agreement with the Canadian Association of Women in Construction (CAWIC).

Canadian Association of Women in Construction

The Canadian Association of Women in Construction (CAWIC) was incorporated as a nonprofit organization in October 2005. It originated twenty-five years ago when a group of Toronto-area professional women working in construction formed the Toronto Chapter 295 of the National Association of Women in Construction (NAWIC). In 2006 CAWIC aligned itself through affiliate agreements with NAWIC in the United States, United Kingdom, South Africa, Australia, and New Zealand.

CAWIC's membership base includes both individuals and companies involved in construction and related fields. Companies include general and specialty contractors, architectural and engineering firms, building product manufacturers and distributors, real estate professionals, interior designers, trade associations, law firms, and other professional service providers.

Individual members include tradeswomen, architects, business owners and executives, estimators, lawyers, engineers, project managers, real estate agents, sales and marketing professionals, and students, too.

The organization publishes a monthly newsletter and job postings. Go to www.cawic.ca for complete information.

Professional Women in Construction

This nonprofit organization began with a dozen women in 1980 as a provider of seminars and networking events. Today it has more than six hundred members, including women, men, companies, and public agencies and represents over eight thousand constituents.

Members come from all corners of the construction industry, including real estate, development, facilities and property management, general and specialty contractors, environmental services, and suppliers of all kinds of goods and services. There are also representatives from law and accounting firms, insurance/surety and bonding companies, banks and financial services, graphic design services, printers, computer consulting firms, travel agencies, and marketing firms. For more information, visit www.pwcusa.org.

Systems-Built Housing

There are a number of current and emerging trends in construction that will have an impact on the future of the building industry. The last few years, for example, have seen an increase in the popularity of systems-built housing across North America. *Systems-built housing* refers to methods of construction that take advantage of modern machinery, computer, and factory technology to create a code-compliant home.

Systems-built homes use prefabricated materials, which are built in a climate-controlled environment and designed to work as a precise system, to complete the home. The categories of systems-built housing are panelized, modular, and log. NAHB's Building Systems Councils represent these producers, builders, and vendors.

Systems-built housing benefits both the builder and consumer. Most building systems offer a reduced construction time, allowing for quicker completion and move-in. Building systems also offer more cost control during the construction process and a high degree of energy efficiency.

Panelized Homes

Panelization is the most widely used form of systems building. In this construction method, housing components are prefabricated in a climate-controlled facility before being shipped to a home site.

The most commonly used panelized components are floors and roof trusses, which are employed by many market builders in order to cut production time.

A panelized home is not the same as a modular home. In general, panelization is one step above stick framing. A builder who stick frames a house has an assortment of lifts of wood delivered to the site, where the crew then cuts and assembles the studs panels that are then tilted up into place and fastened.

In panelization, the manufacturer prebuilds all of the interior and exterior panels and delivers them to the building site for assembly. A panelized home includes floor and roof systems, doors and windows, and shingles or siding. Once the outside of the building is erected, subcontractors can finish the interior work.

Modular Homes

Individual modules, the components of modular homes, are up to 90 percent complete when shipped from the factory to the home site. All walls, flooring, ceilings, stairs, carpeting, and wall finishes are completed in the factory before shipment.

Some manufacturers can assemble modules in one day once the building materials arrive at the factory. Typically, a two-story, twenty-five-hundred-square-foot home can be constructed in a factory in less than a week. This short assembly time is an advantage for home buyers, because it reduces the possibility of weather damage or home site vandalism. Modular homes are also energy efficient, saving owners money over the life of the home. Modular systems can be used to construct homes of any size, and this method of building is becoming increasingly popular. In 2004, nearly forty-three thousand modular homes were constructed in the United States, and one of ten homes built in the Northeast is modular.

Log Homes

Log homes are gaining popularity throughout North America, with more than six hundred log home manufacturers operating in the United States and Canada. These homes are environmentally friendly, because wood's natural characteristics often exceed the minimum specifications of energy codes. Ninety percent of log homes are built with milled logs; the remaining 10 percent are hand crafted, with logs individually crafted by hand tools.

Green Building

Green building is constructing buildings to maximize their use of energy, water, and natural materials. An additional goal is to minimize the negative effects of the building on human health and the environment. These goals are achieved through improved location, design, construction, operation, and maintenance.

Proponents of green building, also called *sustainable building*, have outlined a number of features that can enhance a building's environmental appeal. These include:

- Solar heating system to reduce heating costs
- Radiant heat barriers to reduce heat coming through the ceilings
- High-performance showerheads to conserve water and save on water-heating costs
- Maximized kitchen area with recycling center
- Exterior siding that requires minimal upkeep and does not use wood
- Elimination of dampness and mold conditions in the basement

The U.S. Green Building Council (USGBC) designed the Leadership in Energy and Environmental Design (LEED) green building rating system. LEED is a voluntary rating system that outlines standards for what constitutes a green building. It emphasizes site development, water conservation, energy efficiency, and environmental quality. LEED addresses all building types in all sectors, whether residential, commercial, educational, medical, or industrial. The program promotes green building through project certification, professional accreditation, training, and practical resources, and LEED certification indicates that a building meets environmental standards.

The Canada Green Building Council (CGBC) has implemented LEED Canada, which is an adaptation of the USGBC program and is tailored for Canadian climates, construction practices, and regulations.

Emerging Green Builders

Both USGBC and CGBC sponsor Emerging Green Builders (EGB), a resource for students and young professionals who are interested in working in the green building movement. A candidate for EGB membership must be a student, new professional within five years of graduation, or thirty years of age or younger.

Greenbuild

The Greenbuild International Conference and Expo sponsored by USGBC is an annual conference on high-performance building practices. Thousands of building industry professionals meet to learn about new products, projects, and the latest building research. Greenbuild offers educational sessions, an exhibit hall, and internationally renowned speakers.

A Final Word

This chapter has considered a few of the issues and trends affecting building construction. As you can see, this is an industry that will always have room for growth. The issues of safety and inclusion and the trends of progressive and systems-built construction will continue to be important. As they are addressed, they will lead to future topics that will also provide room for continued research and employment opportunities for those who are interested in this exciting field.

Offices of Apprenticeship

U.S. Department of Labor
Employment and Training Administration,
State Offices of Apprenticeship

Please note that individual websites are not available for these offices. Visit www.doleta.gov/oa/stateoffices.cfm for current e-mail information.

Alabama

USDOL/ETA/OA
Medical Forum Bldg., Rm. 648
950 22nd St. N
Birmingham, AL 35203

Alaska

USDOL/ETA/OA
605 W. 4th Ave., Rm. G-30
Anchorage, AK 99501

Arizona

USDOL/ETA/OA
230 N. 1st Ave., Ste. 510
Phoenix, AZ 85025

Arkansas

USDOL/ETA/OA
Federal Bldg., Rm. 3507
700 W. Capitol St.
Little Rock, AR 72201

California

USDOT/ETA/OA
1301 Clay St., Ste. 1090-N
Oakland, CA 94612-5217

Colorado

USDOT/ETA/OA
U.S. Custom House
721 19th St., Rm. 469
Denver, CO 80202

Connecticut

USDOT/ETA/OA
Federal Bldg.
135 High St., Rm. 367
Hartford, CT 06103

Delaware

USDOT/ETA/OA
Federal Bldg., Lock Box 36
844 King St.
Wilmington, DE 19801

Florida

USDOT/ETA/OA
400 W. Bay St., Ste. 934
P.O. Box 10
Jacksonville, FL 32202

Georgia

USDOL/ETA/OA
61 Forsyth St. SW, Rm. 6T80
Atlanta, GA 30303

Hawaii

USDOT/ETA/OA
300 Ala Moana Blvd., Rm. 5-117
Honolulu, HI 96850

Idaho

USDOT/ETA/OA
1150 N. Curtis Rd., Ste. 204
Boise, ID 83706-1234

Illinois

USDOT/ETA/OA
230 S. Dearborn St., Rm. 656
Chicago, IL 60604

Indiana

USDOT/ETA/OA
Federal Bldg. and U.S. Courthouse
46 E. Ohio St., Rm. 414
Indianapolis, IN 46204

Iowa

USDOT/ETA/OA
210 Walnut St., Rm. 715
Des Moines, IA 50309

Kansas

USDOT/ETA/OA
444 SE Quincy St., Rm. 247
Topeka, KS 66683-3571

Kentucky

USDOT/ETA/OA
Federal Bldg., Rm. 168
600 Martin Luther King Pl.
Louisville, KY 40202

Louisiana

USDOT/ETA/OA
Afton Village Condo, Ste. 133
3535 Sherwood Forest Blvd.
Baton Rouge, LA 70816

Maine

USDOT/ETA/OA
Federal Bldg., Rm. 401
68 Sewall St.
Augusta, ME 04330

Maryland

USDOT/ETA/OA
Federal Bldg., Rm. 430-B
31 Hopkins Plaza
Baltimore, MD 21201

Massachusetts

USDOT/ETA/OA
JFK Federal Bldg., Rm. E-370
Boston, MA 02203

Michigan

USDOT/ETA/OA
315 W. Allegan, Rm. 209
Lansing, MI 48933

Minnesota

USDOT/ETA/OA
316 Robert St., Rm. 134
St. Paul, MN 55101

Mississippi

USDOT/ETA/OA
Federal Bldg., Ste. 515
100 W. Capitol St.
Jackson, MS 39269

Missouri

USDOT/ETA/OA
1222 Spruce St., Rm. 9.102E
Robert A. Young Federal Bldg.
St. Louis, MO 63103

Montana

USDOT/ETA/OA
Federal Office Bldg.
301 S. Park Ave., Rm. 396
Helena, MT 59626-0055

Nebraska

USDOT/ETA/OA
111 S. 18th Plaza, Ste. C-49
Omaha, NE 68102-1322

Nevada

USDOT/ETA/OA
600 S. Las Vegas Blvd., Ste. 510
Las Vegas, NV 89101

New Hampshire

USDOT/ETA/OA
Cleveland Bldg., Rm. 3703
55 Pleasant St.
Concord, NH 03301

New Jersey

USDOT/ETA/OA
485 Rte. 1 S
Bldg. E, 3rd Fl.
Iselin, NJ 08830

New Mexico

USDOL/ETA/OA
500 4th St. NW, Ste. 401
Albuquerque, NM 87102

New York

USDOT/ETA/OA
Leo O'Brien Federal Bldg., Rm. 809
North Pearl and Clinton Ave.
Albany, NY 12207

North Carolina

USDOT/ETA/OA
Somerset Park, Ste. 205
4407 Bland Rd.
Raleigh, NC 27609

North Dakota

USDOT/ETA/OA
304 Broadway, Rm. 332
Bismarck, ND 58501-5900

Ohio

USDOT/ETA/OA
200 N. High St., Rm. 605
Columbus, OH 43215

Oklahoma

USDOT/ETA/OA
1500 S. Midwest Blvd., Ste. 202
Midwest City, OK 73110

Oregon

USDO/ETA/OA
Federal Bldg., Rm. 629
1220 SW 3rd Ave.
Portland, OR 97204

Pennsylvania

USDOT/ETA/OA
Federal Bldg.
228 Walnut St., Rm. 356
Harrisburg, PA 17108

Rhode Island

USDOT/ETA/OA
Federal Bldg.
100 Hartford Ave.
Providence, RI 02909

South Carolina

USDOT/ETA/OA
Strom Thurmond Federal Bldg.
1835 Assembly St., Rm. 838
Columbia, SC 29201

South Dakota

USDOT/ETA/OA
2500 W. 49th St., Rm. 204
Sioux Falls, SD 57105

Tennessee

USDOT/ETA/OA
Airport Executive Plaza
1321 Murfreesboro Rd., Ste. 541
Nashville, TN 37210

Texas

USDOT/ETA/OA
300 E. 8th St., Ste. 914
Austin, TX 78701

Utah

USDOT/ETA/OA
1600 W. 2200 S, Ste. 101
Salt Lake City, UT 84119

Vermont

USDOT/ETA/OA
Federal Bldg.
11 Elmwood Ave., Rm. 629
Burlington, VT 05401

Virginia

USDOT/ETA/OA
Federal Bldg., Ste. 404
400 N. 8th St.
Richmond, VA 23219

Washington

USDOT/ETA/OA
1111 3rd Ave., Ste. 850
Seattle, WA 98101-3212

West Virginia

USDOT/ETA/OA
1 Bridge Pl., 2nd Fl.
Charleston, WV 25301

Wisconsin

USDOT/ETA/OA
740 Regent St., Ste. 104
Madison, WI 53715-1233

Wyoming

USDOT/ETA/OA
American National Bank Bldg.
1912 Capitol Ave., Rm. 508
Cheyenne, WY 82001-3661

Canadian Council of Directors of Apprenticeship, Provincial Offices

Alberta

Apprenticeship and Industry Training
South Tower, 7th Fl.
Capital Health Centre
10030–107 St.
Edmonton, AB
Canada T5J 4X7
www.tradesecrets.org

British Columbia

Industry Training Authority
Ste. 110, 2985 Virtual Way
Vancouver, BC
Canada V5M 4X7
www.itabc.ca

Manitoba

Manitoba Advanced Education and Literacy
310–800 Portage Ave.
Winnipeg, MB
Canada R3G 0N4
www.edu.gov.mb.ca/ael

New Brunswick

Department of Post-Secondary Education, Training,
and Labour Apprenticeship and Certification
P.O. Box 6000
Chestnut Complex
Fredericton, NB
Canada E3B 5H1
www.gnb.ca/0381/0001e.htm

Newfoundland and Labrador

Department of Education
Industrial Training Section
Confederation Bldg., West Block Basement
St. John's, NL
Canada A1B 4J6
www.ed.gov.nl.ca/app

Northwest Territory

Government of the NWT
Education, Culture, and Employment
Apprenticeship and Occupational Certification
P.O. Box 1320
Yellowknife NT
Canada X1A 2L9
www.ece.gov.nt.ca/divisions/apprenticeship/index.htm

Nova Scotia

Department of Education, Apprenticeship Training,
   and Skill Development Division
2021 Brunswick St.
P.O. Box 578
Halifax, NS
Canada B3J 2S9
www.apprenticeship.ednet.ns.ca

Nunavut Territory

Nunavut Arctic College Head Office
P.O. Box 230
Arviat, NT
Canada X0C 0E0
www.nac.nu.ca

Ontario

Ministry of Training, Colleges and Universities
www.edu.gov.on.ca/eng/tcu/apprentices

Prince Edward Island

Apprenticeship Training
Department of Education
Sullivan Bldg., 3rd Fl.
16 Fitzroy St.
Charlottetown, PE
Canada C1A 7N8
www.gov.pe.ca/educ

Saskatchewan

Saskatchewan Apprenticeship and Trade Certification Commission
2140 Hamilton St.
Regina, SK
Canada S4P 2E3
www.saskapprenticeship.gov.sk.ca

Yukon Territory

Department of Education Apprenticeship Training
www.education.gov.yk.ca

Appendix B

Associations and Agencies

THE FOLLOWING ARE trade associations and organizations that can be contacted for information about the trades, trends, and issues discussed in this book.

General Information

Associated Builders and Contractors
4250 N. Fairfax Dr., 9th Fl.
Arlington, VA 22203-1607
www.abc.org

Associated General Contractors of America
2300 Wilson Blvd., Ste. 400
Arlington, VA 22201
www.agc.org

Canadian Home Builders' Association
150 Laurier Ave. W, Ste. 500
Ottawa, ON
Canada K1P 5J4
www.chba.ca

Home Builders Institute
1201 15th St. NW, 6th Fl.
Washington, DC 20005
www.hbi.org

Carpentry and Related Trades

Carpenters

United Brotherhood of Carpenters and Joiners of America
www.carpenters.org

Insulation Workers

Insulation Contractors Association of America
www.insulate.org

International Association of Heat and Frost Insulators
and Asbestos Workers
9602 Martin Luther King Jr. Hwy.
Lanham, MD 20706
www.insulators.org

Plasterers

Operative Plasterers' and Cement Masons' International Association
11720 Beltsville Dr., Ste. 700
Beltsville, MD 20705
www.opcmia.org

Exterior and Interior Trades

Operating Engineers

International Union of Operating Engineers
1125 17th St. NW
Washington, DC 20036
www.iuoe.org

Ironworkers

Ironworkers International
1750 New York Ave. NW, Ste. 400
Washington, DC 20006
www.ironworkers.org

National Association of Reinforcing Steel Contractors
P.O. Box 280
Fairfax, VA 22038
www.narsc.com

Brick Masons, Stonemasons, Tile Setters, Cement and Concrete Masons

Canadian Masonry Contractors Association
Canadian Masonry Centre
360 Superior Blvd.
Mississauga, ON
Canada L5T 2N7
www.canadamasonrycentre.com

International Masonry Institute Apprenticeship and Training
The James Brice House
42 East St.
Annapolis, MD 21401
www.imiweb.org

International Union of Bricklayers and Allied Craftworkers
620 F St. NW
Washington, DC 20004
www.bacweb.org

National Terrazzo and Mosaic Association
201 N. Maple, Ste. 208
Purcellville, VA 20132
www.ntma.org

Operative Plasterers' and Cement Masons' International Association (OPCMIA)
11720 Beltsville Dr., Ste. 700
Beltsville, MD 20705
www.opcmia.org

Portland Cement Association
5420 Old Orchard Rd.
Skokie, IL 60077
www.cement.org

Roofers

Canadian Roofing Contractors Association
2430 Don Reid Dr., Ste. 100
Ottawa, ON
Canada K1H 1E1
www.roofingcanada.com

National Roofing Contractors Association
10255 W. Higgins Rd., Ste. 600
Rosemont, IL 60018-5607
www.nrca.net

United Union of Roofers, Waterproofers, and Allied Workers
1660 L St. NW, Ste. 800
Washington, DC 20036-5646
www.unionroofers.com

Painters and Paperhangers

International Brotherhood of Painters and Allied Trades
1750 New York Ave. NW
Washington, DC 20006
www.iupat.org

Licensed Trades

Electricians

Canadian Electrical Contractors Association
460–170 Attwell Dr.
Toronto, ON
Canada M9W 5Z5
www.ceca.org

Independent Electrical Contractors
4401 Ford Ave., Ste. 1100
Alexandria, VA 22302
www.ieci.org

International Brotherhood of Electrical Workers
900 7th St. NW
Washington, DC 20001
www.ibew.org

National Electrical Contractors Association
3 Bethesda Metro Center, Ste. 1100
Bethesda, MD 20814
www.necanet.org

Plumbers and Pipe Fitters

Canadian Automatic Sprinkler Association
www.casa-firesprinkler.org

National Fire Sprinkler Association
40 Jon Barrett Rd.
Patterson, NY 12563
www.nfsa.org

Plumbing-Heating-Cooling Contractors Association
180 S. Washington St.
P.O. Box 6808
Falls Church, VA 22046
www.phccweb.org

Elevator Installers and Repairers

International Union of Elevator Constructors
7154 Columbia Gateway Dr.
Columbia, MD 21046
www.iuec.org

Sheet Metal Workers

Sheet Metal and Air-Conditioning Contractors'
    National Association
4201 Lafayette Center Dr.
Chantilly, VA 20151-1209
www.smacna.org

Sheet Metal Workers International Association
1750 New York Ave. NW
Washington, DC 20006
www.smwia.org

Heating, Air-Conditioning, and Refrigeration Mechanics and Installers

Air-Conditioning Contractors of America
2800 Shirlington Rd., Ste. 300
Arlington, VA 22206
www.acca.org

Air-Conditioning and Refrigeration Institute
4100 N. Fairfax Dr., Ste. 200
Arlington, VA 22203
www.ari.org

Heating, Refrigeration, and Air-Conditioning Institute of Canada
2800 Skymark Ave., Bldg. 1, Ste. 201
Mississauga, ON
Canada L4W 5A6
www.hrai.ca

Plumbing-Heating-Cooling Contractors Association
180 S. Washington St.
P.O. Box 6808
Falls Church, VA 22046
www.phccweb.org

Refrigeration Service Engineers Society
www.rses.org

Safety Issues

Canadian Centre for Occupational Health and Safety
135 Hunter St. E
Hamilton, ON
Canada L8N 1M5
www.ccohs.ca

U.S. Department of Labor
Occupational Safety and Health Administration
200 Constitution Ave. NW
Washington, DC 20210
www.osha.gov

Women in Construction

Canadian Association of Women in Construction
www.cawic.ca

National Association of Women in Construction
www.nawic.org

Professional Women in Construction
315 E. 56th St.
New York, NY 10022
www.pwcusa.org

Green Building

Canada Green Building Council
325 Dalhousie St., Ste. 800
Ottawa, ON
Canada K1N 7G2
www.cagbc.org

U.S. Green Building Council
1800 Massachusetts Ave. NW, Ste. 300
Washington, DC 20036
www.usgbc.org

About the Authors

Michael Sumichrast was a founding member and chairman of the board of Eastbrokers International Inc. from 1993 to March 1997 and is now retired and living in Potomac, Maryland.

Prior to his tenure at Eastbrokers, Sumichrast was the chief economist and senior vice president of the National Association of Home Builders. His expertise is unique in that he has wide personal building experience for a housing economist; he has built more than three thousand housing units and commercial and industrial buildings in Australia and the United States. Additionally, he served as a consulting engineer in Asia and Latin America.

During the Second World War, Sumichrast served as a lieutenant in the Czechoslovak armed forces, which was a part of the Russian army under Marshall Malinovsky. He is the recipient of two war decorations and a special presidential Michael Kovac medal. Sumichrast was promoted in 1994 to a full colonel in the Slovak army.

Sumichrast studied industrial engineering in Czechoslovakia and received his Ph.D. in economics from Ohio State University. For six years he was a professor at American University in Washington, DC. A writer, lecturer, and researcher, Sumichrast is regarded in academic, government, and business circles as one of the nation's outstanding housing economists.

Sumichrast has had a long history in the Washington area, serving on the equal opportunity and housing advisory committees during the Johnson and Carter administrations and later on the Housing Task Force for George H. W. Bush's 1988 presidential campaign. He served as a member of the 1980 and 1990 decennial censuses and is associated with several other professional organizations. He was also a founding member of the influential Monetary Policy Forum in 1983 and coauthored a syndicated column on national real estate. He was a regular contributor to *The Washington Post* and *Washington Star*.

His book America the Dream Country was published in 1999 by Hellgate Press in Oregon and translated into Slovak in his home country. This book is his story of fighting the Nazis, fleeing the Communists who took over Czechoslovakia in 1948, and eventually starting a new life in the United States in the midst of the Eisenhower recession. Working hard and taking advantage of the enormous opportunities offered to immigrants in the United States, Sumichrast found freedom and eventually success. He also discovered that the American democratic system is still best in the world.

Sumichrast has published more than thirty books, including *The New Complete Book of Home Buying* and *Opportunities in Financial Careers*, as well as numerous studies and articles.

David Davitaia graduated from the University of Maryland in 1999 with a major in criminology and criminal justice. He is currently working toward his master's degree in homeland security management.

Davitaia is an assistant director/general manager for the Department of Transportation Services, responsible for university transit systems and construction and maintenance of parking garages.

The authors would like to thank Josephine Scanlon for her help in revising this edition.